MW00783390

DATE DUE

2-6-2002	
2-7-2002	
2-21-2002	
9-14-04	
9-20-04	
9-23-04	
10-2-04	
10-4-04	
10-21-04	
2-6-2006	
9-19-06	
3-17-07	
Feb 7, 2008	
OCT 1 4 2008	

GAYLORD	PRINTED IN U.S.A.

Authentic
Georgian Furniture
Designs

Authentic Georgian Furniture Designs

Universal System of Household Furniture, 1762

William Ince
and
John Mayhew

DOVER PUBLICATIONS, INC.
Mineola, New York

Published in Canada by General Publishing Company, Ltd., 30 Lesmill Road, Don Mills, Toronto, Ontario.

Published in the United Kingdom by Constable and Company, Ltd., 3 The Lanchesters, 162–164 Fulham Palace Road, London W6 9ER.

Bibliographical Note

This Dover edition, first published in 1998, is an unabridged republication of the work originally published in London in 1762 under the title *The Universal System of Household Furniture.*

Library of Congress Cataloging-in-Publication Data

Ince, William.
  Authentic Georgian furniture designs : universal system of household furniture, 1762 / William Ince and John Mayhew.
        p.   cm.
  Originally published: The universal system of household furniture. London : Ince & Mayhew, 1762?.
  ISBN 0-486-40295-9 (pbk.)
  1. Furniture, Georgian. 2. Furniture design—England. I. Mayhew, John. II. Ince, William. Universal system of household furniture.   III. Title.
NK2528.I53   1998
749.22—dc21   98-26517
                                                                                                    CIP

Manufactured in the United States of America
Dover Publications, Inc., 31 East 2nd Street, Mineola, N.Y. 11501

The

Universal System

of

HOUSHOLD FURNITURE.

Consisting of above 300 Designs in the most elegant taste, both useful & Ornamental Finely Engraved, in which the nature of Ornament & Perspective, is accurately exemplified. The Whole made convenient to the Nobility and Gentry, in their choice, & comprehensive to the Workman, by directions for executing the several Designs, with specimens of Ornament for Young Practitioners in Drawing.

By

Ince & Mayhew

CABINET-MAKERS & UPHOLDERS,

in Broad Street, Golden Square, London. Where Every Article in the several Branches treated, of is executed on the most reasonable terms, with the utmost neatness & punctuality.

W. Ince inv.t et delin.

Sold by Rob.t Sayer Map & Printseller near Serjeants Inn, Fleet Street.

Le

Systeme Universel

de

GARNITURE de MAISON,

Contenant.

plus de trois Cens Desseins, du Gout le
plus elegant tant pour l'Utilité que pour
l'Ornement, Compilé pour l'assistance des
Messieurs dans leur Choix et des Ouvriers
dans l'execution des Meubles, dans le
quel la Nature de l'Ornement est am-
plement montrée par des Examples.

Par

Ince & Mayhew

Ebenistes et Tapissiers,
dans Broad street, prés de Golden square,
à Londres.

DIEU · DEFEND · LE DROIT

To
the most Noble
George Spencer,
DUKE of MARLBOROUGH, MARQUIS of BLANDFORD,
Earl of Sunderland and Marlborough,
Baron Spencer of Wormleighton, & Baron Churchill of Sundridge ;
Lord Lieutenant & CUSTOS ROTULORUM of the County of Oxford & Lord Chamberlain of his
Majesties Houshold &c.

May it please Your Grace

Being sensible of Your Grace's extensive
Knowledge, in the Arts & Sciences, but more particularly in Drawing and, Your being
ever willing to promote, and encourage Industry & Ingenuity, will justly account for our
presumption in claiming the protection of so worthy a Patron to this Work, which if so fortu-
nate as to merit Your GRACE'S approbation will be esteem'd as the greatest Honour
ever conferred on

Your Graces,
most Respectful,
most Obedient,
and very faithful Serv.ts
Mayhew & Ince

PREFACE.

PREFACES like Titles are only meant as an Argument to the Reader, but when too long, grow tedious, and are feldom read half through; to prevent which fhall be concife, and only fay, that the very few Publications that has been produced of this Nature, with many Intreaties of our feveral Friends, induced us to compile the following Defigns, tho' not without much Controverfy in our own Opinions; as Effects of this Nature are ever Suffrages of Public Criticifm, efpecially among the Degree of thofe Artifts which the Subject tends to: But with refpect to the judicious Part of Mankind, we are certain they are ever Friends to the Induftrious, and their Candour will at leaft, if not look over, excufe thofe Faults which can only be attributed to the early Endeavours of fuch an Undertaking.

Notwithftanding the CABINET and UPHOLSTERY Branch is at prefent raifed to a very high Pitch, as we daily fee by the many elegant Pieces of Work now made, and the prefent furnifhing of fome capital Houfes, tho' by Obfervation may be perceived in fome great Abfurdities, which might eafily be avoided if managed by an ingenious Workman.

In Furnifhing all fhould be with Propriety. --- Elegance fhould always be joined with a peculiar Neatnefs through the whole Houfe, or otherwife an immenfe Expence may be thrown away to no Purpofe, either in Ufe or Appearance; and with the fame Regard any Gentleman may furnifh as neat at a fmall Expence, as he can elegant and fuperb at a great one.   We

We have endeavoured to make this Work as familiar as poffible to every Individual, and in Order to render it of a more material Confequence to thofe whofe Ingenuity would lead them to Proficiency, have firft entered on the true Rudiments of Ornament, without which none can arrive to that Perfection neceffary in the Cabinet Branch, the principal Part of which being fo blended with Ornament, as its proper Decoration in both neat and capital Pieces of Work.

In the Cabinet Work have been particularly careful to place every Dimenfion neceffary, and Remarks in the Plates to render the Explanation as eafy as poffible to the Capacity of every Workman, moft of which have the Mouldings at large defcribed, with their Ornaments affixed on the fame Plate; and as it is too often the Cafe, that a great Expence fruftrates the Means of a good Defign bringing itfelf to publick Utility, have contrived to avoid that, by engraving thofe Pieces of Furniture moft ufeful, and filling up the Plates more than ever we at firft intended; by which Means are enabled to reduce them to fuch a Number as may render the Expence more fuitable to every Purchafer.

E X-

EXPLANATION	EXPLICATION
OF THE	DES
PLATES.	**PLANCHES.**

PLATE I.

CONTAINING several Pieces of Foliage properly adapted to young beginners in their first practice of Drawing, being extremely necessary to bring the Hand into that Freedom required in all kind of Ornament, useful to Carvers, Cabinet-Makers, Chasers, Engravers, &c. &c. The Learner must Observe to begin with the Centre-Lines first, and then proceed to form the Out-Lines.

PLATE II.

Is a compleat Leaf of Foliage; the principal Sweep or Centre Line is the Foundation and Basis of the whole Order of Ornament; that must be first drawn and made perfect (which can only be done by freedom of Hand) before you proceed any further; then form the other Centre-Lines, which must all spring with a natural Freedom from the first or principal Sweep, all which must be perfectly correct before any other Attempts are made; then form the several Out-Lines by lightly sketching them in with the Pencil, so as to bring the Whole into its proper Form, with exact Proportion, which is the grand Point; all which being done, proceed to strengthen the Out-Lines, draw the Veins and Shades, keeping the right Hand darkest: For young beginners it would be better to take any Part, and by degrees be able to manage the Whole.

PLATE III.

Is another of the same kind, in which the Rule in the last must be observed.

A   PLATE

PLANCHE I.

CONTIENT diverses parties de feuillages adaptés à la capacité des jeunes gens qui commencent à s'exercer dans le dessein ; ces feuillages deviennent extrêmement nécessaires pour faire acquerir à la main toute la liberté et la hardiesse dont elle a besoin dans ce genre d'Ornemens, et ils sont de la plus grande utilité aux Sculpteurs, Ebénistes, Ciseleurs, Graveurs, &c. &c. L'Etudiant doit avoir l'attention de commencer d'abord par les Lignes du milieu, et de venir ensuite à la formation des contours extérieurs.

PLANCHE II.

Représente une feuille complete. la *Côte* principale ou Ligne du milieu est la base sur la quelle est fondé l'Ordre entier de l'Ornement. Cette ligne se tracera la première de toutes, et on ne doit point la quitter que son contour ne soit parfait, (ce qui ne se peut faire qu'en ayant la main Libre et hardie). On formera ensuite les autres Lignes de milieu qui doivent toutes sortir Naturellement de cette première ou principale *Côte* ; et on aura pareillement l'attention de rechercher leur contour avec toute la correction possible. Lorsque toutes ces lignes seront achevées, on tracera les traits extérieurs en les esquissant légèrement au crayon, et on aménera insensiblement tout l'Ouvrage à la forme qu'il doit avoir, en observant l'exactitude des proportions, ce qui est le point essenciel. Cette esquisse finie, on donnera des coups de force aux traits extérieurs ; on marquera les veines et les ombres, ayant soin de tenir le côté droit plus obscur. Il seroit mieux pour les commençans de n'entreprendre qu'une partie, afin de se rendre par degrés en état de conduire le tout.

PLANCHE III.

Est une autre feuille du même genre, dans le dessein de la quelle les régles que l'on vient de prescrire doivent etre observées.

PLANCHE

PLATE IV.

Is three Hall Chairs in the Gothic Taste, the Ornaments of which, if thought too Expensive, may be painted, and have a very good Effect.

PLATE V.

Is two Hall Lanthorns, the first is an Hexagon in the Gothic Taste, and would have a very good Effect; the other Square, with French Ornaments.

PLATE VI.

Is two other Designs, calculated for being made in Brass or Wood; of the latter we have executed some which are much admired, and at a much less Expence than Brass.

PLATE VII.

Is six different Designs for Stair-Case Lights, mostly designed to fix on the Hand Rail.

PLATE VIII.

Is four Designs for Therms, to support Busts or Lamps.

PLATE IX.

Is four Designs for Parlour Chairs, with different Patterns for Legs.

PLATE X.

Is four other Designs of Parlour Chairs.

PLATE XI.

Is four different Designs for Sideboard Tables; the Mouldings are at large, and a Scale to them.

PLATE XII.

Is two other Designs for Sideboards.

PLATE XIII.

Three very neat Designs for Claw-Tables.

PLATE XIV.

Eight Designs for Tea-kettle Stands.

PLANCHE IV.

Trois Chaises ou Fauteuils dans le goût gothique, pour un Vestibule. si l'Ornement en paroissoit trop dispendieux, on pourroit peindre ces Fauteuils, et ils feroient un tres bel effet.

PLANCHE V.

Deux Lanternes pour un Vestibule. La première est un Exagone dans le goût Gothique et feroit d'un bel effet. L'autre est Quadrangulaire avec des ornemens à la Françoise.

PLANCHE VI.

Deux autres Desseins faits pour être exécutés en cuivre ou en bois. Nous en avons exécutés de cette dernière sorte quelques uns que l'on a beaucoup admirés et qui coutent bien moins qu'en cuivre.

PLANCHE VII.

Six Desseins différens pour des Flambeaux d'escalier, la plûpart destinés à être placés sur la Balustrade.

PLANCHE VIII.

Quatre Desseins de Termes pour supporter des Bustes ou des Lampes.

PLANCHE IX.

Quatre Desseins de Chaises pour une salle de compagnie, avec différens Modéles pour les Pieds.

PLANCHE X.

Quatre autres Desseins de Chaises pour une salle de Compagnie.

PLANCHE XI.

Quatre Desseins différens de Cabarets; les Moulures font en grand et on y a mis une échelle.

PLANCHE XII.

Deux autres Desseins de Cabarets.

PLANCHE XIII.

Trois Desseins élégans de Tables-à-un-seul-pied.

PLANCHE XIV.

Huit Desseins de Supports de Bouilloirs-à-Thé.
PLANCHE

PLATE XV.

Four Defigns for Trays or Voiders.

PLATE XVI.

A Defign for a Defk and Book-Cafe on a Frame; the Doors for Glafs; the Legs to be cut through; the Infide of the Defk is annext to the Defign.

PLATE XVII.

A Defk and Book-cafe in Perfpective, with Glafs Doors; the Fall to be let down with a Quadrant at A; the Infide defcribed at the Bottom B; the Mouldings at large, and a Scale to the Defign.

PLATE XVIII.

Two Ladies Secretaries; the firft is in the Gothic Tafte, with Glafs Doors; the other is intended to be open, and may have a green Silk Curtain; the Defk Part draws out, and when up, fhews Draws to the Top.

PLATE XIX.

Two Book-cafes intended for Receffes, their Mouldings are at large, and a Scale to the Defign.

PLATE XX.

A large Book-cafe for a Library or Side of a Room.

PLATE XXI.

A Gentleman's Repofitory; the upper Part or Middle is a Book-cafe; on each Side is Draws; the Top of the under Part or Middle, is a Defk Drawer; under that either Draws or Cloaths-Prefs, as fhewn by two Defigns; on each Side Cupboards.

PLATE XXII.

Two Defigns of Library Steps; the Firft intended for a large Room; E is the Plan of the Scrole for the Hand Rail; the other contrived (for little Room) to fold up; at A A are two Braces of Iron, which keeps out the Sides to a Proper Square, and kept up by two Springs; at

A 2

PLANCHE XV.

Quatre Deffeins de Paniers-à-deffervir.

PLANCHE XVI.

Deffeins d'un Pupître et d'une Armoire-à-livres fur un chaffis. les battants font de glaçe et les pieds font repercés pour montrer la decoupure. l'intérieur du Pupître eft joint au deffein.

PLANCHE XVII.

Deffein en Perfpective d'un Pupître et d'un Armoire-à-livres avec des battants de glaçe. la partie qui s'abbat joue fur un quart de Cercle A. l'intérieur eft décrit au bas de la Planche B, et les Moulures font en grand avec une échelle.

PLANCHE XVIII.

Deux *Sécrétaires* pour femme. le premier eft dans le goût Gothique avec un battant de glaçe. l'autre eft deftiné à être ouvert et peut avoir au devant un rideau de foye verte. la partie qui forme le Pupître fe tire en dehors, et lorfqu'elle eft levée, préfente des tiroirs jufqu'au haut.

PLANCHE XIX.

Deux Armoires-à-livres deftinées pour des, Embrazures. Leurs Moulures font en grand, et il y a une échelle au Deffein.

PLANCHE XX.

Grande Armoire-à-livres pour plaçer dans une Bibliothéque, où pour garnir le côté d'une chambre.

PLANCHE XXI.

Armoire pour homme. Dans la partie fupérieure du milieu eft une Armoire féparée pour les livres, avec des tiroirs de chaque côté. La partie inférieure du milieu eft un Pupître en tiroir, et fous ce pupître d'autres tiroirs ou des garderobes, ainfi qu'on le voit dans le Deffein. De chaque côté font des Buffets.

PLANCHE XXII.

Deux Deffeins d'Echelles où Marche-pieds pour des Bibliothéques. La premiere eft deftinée pour une grande falle. E, eft le Plan du Rouleau qui forme la Baluftrade. La feconde qui convient à de petits appartemens eft faite pour fe plier; Aux endroits marqués A, A, il y a deux

C C

crampons

C C are the Centres to the Steps; at D D the Stays to keep them to a proper Spread; and F shews the Plan when folded up.

PLATE XXIII.

Two Library Tables with their Mouldings at large.

PLATE XXIV.

Two Writing Tables with double rising Tops; the different Positions of the last are expressed by the Out-lines at A A A and B B B; at C is shewn how the Slider comes against the Part of the Front which falls down for the Conveniency of leaving Papers, &c. on the Slider, when shut. They are both drawn in Perspective; the Eye is the Point of Sight for both, and on the same Line mark of eight Feet each way for the Point of Distance.

PLATE XXV.

A Study or Writing Table, with a writing Drawer; at *a d* is the Part of the Front which falls down, to give room for Books or Papers on the Slider; at A B C D are Holes for Papers; the Mouldings are at large; *b* is the Fret on the Drawer Front, and C a Quadrant Standish.

PLATE XXVI.

Five Reading or Music Desks; the Middle one is on a Stand; the Tops fall down upon one another; at *A* is a Brass Quadrant Candlestick, and takes off; at *B B* are other Conveniencies for Candlesticks, which turns under; at *C* is a Rack which raises the Desk to any height by a Thumb Spring.

PLATE XXVII.

A Bed to appear as a Soffa, with a fixt Canopy over it; the Curtains draws on a Rod; the Cheeks and Seat takes off to open the Bedstead; *A* shews the Bedstead when folded up, and the Box under for putting the Bedding; at *B* is the Bedstead shewn as let down.

crampons de fer qui assujétissent les côtés à la forme quarrée nécessaire, et qui sont retenus à C, C, pardeux ressorts. à D, D, ils s'arrêtent pour tenir les dégrés dans le développement convenable. F, fait voir le Plan de ces dégrés pliés.

PLANCHE XXIII.

Deux Tables de Bibliothéque avec leurs Moulures en grand.

PLANCHE XXIV.

Deux Tables-à-écrire avec des doubles-dessus qui se lévent. Les diverses positions de ces dessus sont exprimées par des traits marqués aux endroits A, A, A, & B, B, B; à C, on voit de quelle maniére le Glissoir vient aboutir contre la partie de devant. Cette partie s'abbat afin que l'on aye la commodité de pouvoir plaçer des papiers &c. sur le Glissoir lors qu'il est fermé. Ces deux Tables sont représentées l'une et l'autre en Perspective. L'œil est le point de vue pour toutes les deux; et sur la même ligne, le point de Distançe se trouvera marqué à 8 pieds de chaque côté.

PLANCHE XXV.

Etude ou Table-à-écrire, avec un tiroir dont on peut se servir pour écrire. à *a d*, est la partie de devant qui s'abbat pour laisser de la plaçe aux livres ou aux papiers sur le Glissoir; à A,B,C,D, il y a des ouvertures pratiquées pour serrer des Papiers. Les Moulures sont en grand; *b* est la Découpure sur le devant du Tiroir, et C, est une Ecritoire qui joue sur un quart de Cercle.

PLANCHE XXVI.

Cinq Pupîtres de Musique ou de Lecture. Celui du milieu est sur un Support, et ses dessus s'abbattent l'un sur l'autre. à l'endroit marqué, *A*, est un Chandelier sur un quart de cercle en cuivre, lequel peut s'oter; à *B, B*, il y a d'autres commodités pour des Chandeliers, que l'on tourne en dessous; à *C* est placée une *dentelure* en forme de cric, qui sert à élever le Pupître à diverses hauteurs, au moyen d'un ressort que l'on conduit avec le pouçe.

PLANCHE XXVII.

Lit qui paroit comme un Sopha, avec un Dais fixe au dessus; les Rideaux se tirent sur une Tringle, et les côtés ainsi que le dessus s'enlévent pour ouvrir le Bois de lit. *A*, fait voir le Bois de lit lorsqu'il est plié, et le Coffre placé au dessous pour y renfermer les couvertures, courtepointes &c. à *B*, on voit le Bois de lit tel qu'il paroit lorsqu'il est abbatu.

PLATE XXVIII.

Is a Couch or Bed occafionally; the Teafter being to take off, and conceal'd in the Recefs, under the Seat; at *b A* is the Side of the Teafter Laths, which has a Joint Hinge; *B B B B* fhows the Front; *C* is a Top to the Seat which lifts up; at *E E* the Pofts and Cornice fixt on the Laths; *D* the Bottom to hold the Furniture, &c. *F* the Head, &c.

PLATE XXIX.

A Bed; the Head-board for covering the Curtain to draw on a Rod.

PLATE XXX.

A Bed proper for an Alcove; the Ornaments may be either gilt or cover'd with Damafk; the manner of forming the Teafter is defcribed by the Plan under the Defign.

PLATE XXXI.

A French Bed, with Fronts each way; an Iron from the Pofts concealed by the carv'd Ornament fupports the Canopy.

PLATE XXXII.

A State Bed, with a Dome Teafter, which has been executed, and may be efteemed amongft the beft in England; the Furniture was blue Damafk, and all the Ornaments in burnifh'd Gold, and richly Fringed; the infide and outfide of the Teafter are differently formed; it is drawn to an inch Scale.

PLATE XXXIII.

Three Night Tables; the Middle one is intended to be lined with Silk, to fhow the Frets; the other has its Top to rife for reading.

PLATE XXXIV.

Six Defigns for Dreffing Stools.

PLATE XXXV.

Four Defigns of Dreffing Chairs.

PLATE XXXVI.

Two Defigns of Toilets.

PLATE

PLANCHE XXVIII.

Couchette ou lit d'Occafion. Le Ciel de ce lit s'enléve et le cache dans un fond ménagé fous le Siege. à *b*, *A*, eft le Côté des tringles du ciel qui ont un pivot commun. *B, B, B, B,* fait voir le devant. *C*, eft le deffus du fiége et peut fe hauffer. à *E,E*, les Colonnes et la Corniche fixées fur les tringles. *D*, le fond où fe renferment les couvertures &c. *F*, le Doffier &c.

PLANCHE XXIX.

Lit dont le Doffier fe tire fur une tringle, pour couvrir les rideaux.

PLANCHE XXX.

Lit qui convient à une alcove. Les ornemens peuvent etre dorés ou couverts de damas. La manière dont on forme le Ciel eft décrite dans le plan au deffous du deffein.

PLANCHE XXXI.

Lit à la françoife qui fait façe des deux côtés. un fer qui fort des colonnes du lit, et qui fe trouve caché par les ornemens de fculpture, en foutient l'Impériale.

PLANCHE XXXII.

Lit de parade avec un ciel en forme de dôme. Ce lit a eté exécuté et peut être mis au nombre des plus beaux qui foyent en Angleterre. La garniture etoit d'un damas bleu, et tous les ornemens d'Or bruni, avec des franges très riches. Le dedans et le dehors du Ciel ont chacun une forme différente, et le tout eft deffiné fur une échelle d'un pouçe au pied.

PLANCHE XXXIII.

Trois Tables de nuit. Celle du milieu doit etre doublée de foye pour faire voir les cifelures l'autre a un deffus qui fe hauffe et fur le quel on peut lire.

PLANCHE XXXIV.

Six Deffeins de Tabourets de toilette.

PLANCHE XXXV.

Quatre Deffeins de Chaifes de toilette.

PLANCHE XXXVI.

Deux Deffeins de Toilettes.

B   PLANCHE

PLATE XXXVII.

A Ladies Toilet, with Drawers under the Glaſs; intended either for Japan or burniſh'd Gold.

PLATE XXXVIII.

Two Dreſſing Tables, with their full Apparatus.

PLATE XXXIX.

Another Dreſſing Table, and contrived for writing alſo; the Drawer is explained by its Plan; at A is a Quadrant Drawer for Ink; at B is Diviſions for Bottles; at C are Diviſions for ſmall Boxes; at D are Parts with Covers only; at E is the Dreſſing Glaſs; a Slider goes over the whole Drawer.

PLATE XL.

Is a Gentlemans Dreſſing Table; the Top is fixt by a Quadrant; the Glaſs in a Frame; on the Plan is deſcribed the Baſon, Bottles, Razors, Boxes, &c. at the Ends are Cupboards.

PLATE XLI.

Two Commode Dreſſing Tables; in the firſt at *A a* the Top lifts up, and has the Dreſſing Glaſs in it; *B* is the Plan deſcribing the Diviſions; at *C* is the Plan of the other Commode, the Ornaments of which may be either Braſs or Wood gilt.

PLATE XLII.

Two Tables with each of the Ends different in their Deſigns, either of which if well executed muſt be very elegant.

PLATE XLIII.

A Commode which has been executed from the Plate, and much admired.

PLATE XLIV.

Two Deſigns of Cloaths Cheſts.

PLATE XLV.

Three Book or China Shelves; the middle one intended for Glaſs.

PLATE

PLANCHE XXXVII.

Toilette de femme, avec des tiroirs au deſſous de la glaçe, deſtinée à etre miſe en vernis, ou en Or bruni.

PLANCHE XXXVIII.

Deux Tables de toilette avec tout leur aſſortiment.

PLANCHE XXXIX.

Autre Table de toilette, imaginée pour ſervir en même tems de Table à ecrire. Le tiroir ſe trouve expliqué dans ſon plan. à l'endroit marqué A, eſt placé un tiroir quarré qui ſert d'écritoire. à B, ſont des compartimens pour des fioles. à C. d'autres compartimens pour de petites boètes. à D, ſont des parties qui n'ont qu'un ſimple couvercle. à E, eſt le miroir de toilette, un Gliſſoir couvre tout le tiroir.

PLANCHE XL.

Toilette pour homme. Le deſſus eſt fixe au moyen d'un quart de cercle, et le miroir ſe hauſſe dans un cadre. Dans le plan on peut voir la diſpoſition de la jatte, des fioles, Boètes &c. aux extrêmités ſont des Buffets.

PLANCHE XLI.

Deux Tables de toilette en forme de Commodes. dans la premiere à *A a*, le deſſus ſe léve et renferme le miroir. *B*, eſt le plan qui fait voir les compartimens. *C* eſt le plan de l'autre Commode dont les ornemens peuvent être de cuivre ou de bois doré.

PLANCHE XLII.

Deux Tables dont les extrêmités préſentent chacune un deſſein différent. Ces Tables bien exécutées feront d'un effet très élégant.

PLANCHE XLIII.

Commode que l'on a exécutée d'après ce deſſein, et qui a beaucoup plûe.

PLANCHE XLIV.

Deux Deſſeins d'Armoires pour garderobes.

PLANCHE XLV.

Trois Tablettes pour plaçer des livres ou des porcelaines. Celle du milieu eſt deſtinée pour des Criſtaux.

PLANCHE

PLATE XLVI.

A China Table and Shelf over it for Books or China; at *A* is the Plan of the Bottom, and at *B* the Plan of the Upper Part.

PLATE XLVII.

Two corner Shelves, the second of which has been executed from the Plate; the Sides or back Part to the Shelves were lined with Glass silver'd.

PLATE XLVIII.

A China Case for Japaning, the inside all of Looking-glass, in that manner it has been executed, and has a very elegant effect.

PLATE XLIX.

Another China Case for Japaning.

PLATE L.

Four Designs of Fire Screens.

PLATE LI.

Six Designs of Pedestals or Stands for China Jars or Figures; the upper one has been executed to hold a Jar and two Beakers.

PLATE LII.

Two Designs of Card Tables in Perspective; to the upper one are the Lines of putting it in Perspective, the Point of sight is set off at six Feet six Inches Distance, but may be at seven Feet six, or more, at discretion; the Rules are the same as observed in the next Plate; at *A* is shewn the folding Frame; and at *B* the Slider or Drawer for the Cards.

PLATE LIII.

Two Card Tables; the first has its proper Perspective Lines, which in order to effect, draw the Ground Line marked 1, next the Horizontal Line 2, five Feet six Inches high from the Ground Line, and at eight Feet Distance set off the Point of Sight and Point of Distance, then mark off three Feet on the Ground Line (which gives the two front Legs within about a Foot from the Uprights of the Point of Distance) next draw the Lines 3 and 4, and where they intersect

PLANCHE XLVI.

Table-a-porçelaines avec une tablette au dessus pour des livres, ou d'autres porçelaines. *A*, fait voir le plan du bas, et *B*, Celui du haut.

PLANCHE XLVII.

Deux *Coins* ou Tablettes d'encoignures, dont la seconde a été exécutée d'après ce dessein. les Côtés ou le derriére jusqu' aux Tablettes étoient doublés de verre argenté.

PLANCHE XLVIII.

Buffet-à-porçelaines pour vernisser. l'Intérieur est entiérement de glaçes-à-miroir. On a exécuté un buffet de cette manière, et il faisoit un effet très élégant.

PLANCHE XLIX.

Autre Buffet-à-porçelaines pour vernisser.

PLANCHE L.

Quatre Desseins d'écrans.

PLANCHE LI.

Six Desseins de Piédestaux ou Guéridons pour plaçer des vases ou des figures de porçelaine. Le piédestal d'enhaut a été exécuté pour supporter un Vase et deux Pots.

PLANCHE LII.

Deux Desseins en perspective de Tables-à-Jouer. à celle d'enhaut sont les lignes qui ont servi à traçer la perspective. Le point de vue est placé à six pieds six pouçes de distançe, mais il pourroit etre à sept pieds six pouçes ou même d'avantage à discrétion. Les régles sont les mêmes que celles que l'on a observées dans la planche qui suit. à *A*, l'on voit le cadre pliant et à *B*, le Glissoir ou tiroir pour les cartes.

PLANCHE LIII.

Deux tables-à-jouer. La première a les lignes qui ont servi à la mettre en perspective et voici la manière dont on a procédé. Tirez la ligne de terre marquée, (1) ensuite la ligne horizontale (2). à 5 pieds 6 pouçes au dessus de la ligne de terre, et à 8 pieds de distançe, fixez le point de vue et le point de distançe. Marquez ensuite 3 pieds sur la ligne de terre, ce qui vous donnera les deux pieds de devant de la Table, à environ un pied des à-plombs du point de distançe.

interſect ſtands the other Legs ; then draw the Line parellel to the Ground Line, and the other Leg. *a b c* are Lines drawn at the Top for marking out the Shapes of the Table top. This Method is moſt eaſy to any Capacity, and ſooneſt attainable. The other is a traydrill Table.

PLATE LIV.

Is a Deſign of an Organ Caſe, the middle of the bottom Part is propoſed to take off, in which is the Keys, as ſhewn under ; at A B C, &c. are the Stops.

PLATE LV.

Four Deſigns of Back Stool Chairs ; the laſt has been executed in burniſh'd Gold, from the Plate, and covered with blue Damaſk.

PLATE LVI.

Four more Deſigns of Back Stools.

PLATE LVII

Two Deſigns of corner Chairs or Settees.

PLATE LVIII, and LIX.

Four French Elbow Chairs.

PLATE LX.

Two Deſigns of Birjairs, or half Couches, the Back of the lower one, is made to fall down at pleaſure, by that and the Elbows going in a Centre, and a Pin to go through the Elbow in the Holes marked.

PLATE LXI.

Deſigns of Stools for receſſes of Windows.

PLATE LXII.

Two Deſigns of Soffa's

PLATE LXIII.

An Alcove ornamented in the Gothic Taſte ; with a Soffa adapted to the whole Side of a Room.

PLATE

diſtançe, puis tirez les lignes (3) et (4), et à leur point d'interſection vous aurez les pieds de derriére. Tirez alors la ligne parallèle à la ligne de terre ainſi que l'autre pied. *a, b, c,* ſont des lignes tirées au haut, pour marquer la forme du deſſus de la Table. Cette méthode qui eſt des plus aiſées eſt auſſi celle que l'on apprendra le plus facilement. Le ſecond Deſſein repréſente une Table à *Tri.*

PLANCHE LIV.

Deſſein d'un Buffet d'Orgues. Le milieu de la partie inférieure eſt deſtinée à s'oter. Dans ce milieu ſe voit le Clavier, et à A, B, C, &c. ſont les. . . . .

PLANCHE LV.

Quatre Deſſeins de Chaiſes-à-dos. La dernière à été exécutée; elle étoit dorée d'Or moulu et bruni, et couverte de damas bleu.

PLANCHE LVI.

Quatre autres Deſſeins de Chaiſes-à-dos.

PLANCHE LVII.

Quatre Deſſeins de Chaiſes ou Siéges d'encoignure.

PLANCHE LVIII, et LIX.

Quatre Deſſeins de Chaiſes-à-bras à la Françoiſe.

PLANCHE LX.

Quatre deſſeins de Fauteuils de repos ou Demi-Chaiſes-longues. Le dos du fauteuil qui eſt au bas de la planche peut s'incliner à volonté de manière qu'il rentre avec les bras dans un même centre, et il y a une cheville qui paſſe au travers du bras dans les trous qu'on a exprimés.

PLANCHE LXI.

Deſſeins de Tabourets pour des Embraſures de Fenêtres.

PLANCHE LXII.

Deux Deſſeins de Sophas.

PLANCHE LXIII.

Alcove décorée dans le goût gothique, avec un Sopha fait de manière qu'il peut s'adapter à tout le côté d'une chambre.

PLANCHE

PLATE LXIV.

Is a single headed Couch, which if the Ornaments of the Frame are well carved will be very handsome.

PLATE LXV.

Expresses an Alcove with whole side of a Room described, fitted up compleat with Cushions in form of a Turkish Soffa, a Drapery Curtain in Front, and Girandoles on each Side.

PLATE LXVI.

A rich Candlestick or Girandole, which if executed in Wood gilt, in burnish'd Gold, or Brass, would be extremely grand, and might be equally the same executed in Silver, proper for a Stand or Marble Table.

PLATE LXVII.

Three Candlestands; the first of which is intended for White and Gold, or Japan; the others for Gilding.

PLATE LXVIII.

Four other Designs for Candlestands; the first has been executed in Japan, the second likewise in burnish'd Gold, and has very good Effects.

PLATE LXIX.

Four more Candlestands; the third of which has gained great Applause in the execution; the last would certainly have as good an appearance in work.

PLATE LXX.

Three Designs for Girandoles; two of which has been executed from this Plate since engraved.

PLATE LXXI.

Four other Designs for Girandoles; that of the Story of Phæton is meant to have Glass cut in the Manner it is engraved, the several Rays of which will reflect the Candles in so many different Colours as to render it very beautiful.

PLATE

PLANCHE LXIV.

Lit de repos à simple dossier. si les Ornemens du cadre sont bien sculptés, ce lit a grande apparençe.

PLANCHE LXV.

Alcove, avec tout le côté d'une chambre garni en entier de coussins en maniere d'Estrade turque. au devant est un rideau rattaché dans le milieu et des Girandoles de chaque côté.

PLANCHE LXVI.

Riche Chandelier ou Girandole. si cette piéce etoit exécutée en cuivre, ou en bois doré d'Or bruni, elle auroit la plus grande apparençe. On pourroit aussi la travailler en argent et la faire servir de Guéridon, ou de support à une table de marbre.

PLANCHE LXVII.

Trois Guéridons. Le premier est destiné pour etre exécuté en blanc et en Or, ou pour etre vernissé. Les deux autres sont pour être dorés.

PLANCHE LXVIII.

Quatre autres Desseins de Guéridons. Le premier a eté exécuté en vernis, et le second en Or bruni. ils font l'un et l'autre un très bon effet.

PLANCHE LXIX.

Quatre autres Guéridons. L'exécution du troisiéme a eté extrêmement goutée, et il est certain que le dernier n'auroit pas moins d'apparence s'il etoit exécuté.

PLANCHE LXX.

Trois Desseins de Girandoles, dont deux ont eté exécutées d'après ce dessein, que l'on a gravé depuis.

PLANCHE LXXI.

Deux autres desseins de Girandoles. dans celle qui représente l'Histoire de Phaéton, on a imaginé d'avoir des Cristaux taillés de la maniere dont le dessein est gravé. Les divers rayons de ces Cristaux réfléchiroient les bougies en autant de Couleurs différentes et formeroient un coup d'œil très agréable.

C   PLANCHE

PLATE LXXII.

Two Defigns for Chandeliers; the firft is meant to reprefent a Temple, and each lined with Glafs, and may be executed in Wood and burnifh'd Gold; the laft has been work'd, and looks very grand.

PLATE LXXIII.

Two Defigns for Slab Frames, in Piers under Glaffes.

PLATE LXXIV.

Two other Defigns for Slab Frames.

PLATE LXXV.

Two other Defigns for Slab Frames, both of which muft be very elegant and grand, work'd by the Hand of an ingenious Carver.

PLATE LXXVI.

Eight Defigns of Brackets for Candles or Bufts.

PLATE LXXVII.

Eight Defigns of Frames for Convex or Concave Glaffes, which have a very pretty Effect in a well furnifh'd Room.

PLATE LXXVIII.

Two Defigns of Frames for Oval Glaffes.

PLATE LXXIX.

Four Defigns of Architectoral Frames for Glaffes.

PLATE LXXX.

Two Defigns of Frames for Pier Glaffes, with Borders all round; both which have been executed from the Plate in burnifh'd Gold, and make a handfome appearance.

PLATE LXXXI.

Two Defigns of Architectoral Pier Frames, with Glafs Borders.

PLATE

PLANCHE LXXII.

Deux Deffeins de Candélabres. Le premier eft imaginé pour repréfenter un Temple; et ils font l'un et l'autre revêtus de glaces et peuvent être exécutés en bois et en Or bruni. Le dernier a eté exécuté et fait beaucoup d'apparençe.

PLANCHE LXXIII.

Deux deffeins de Cadres ou Bordures pour des Tables à placer au deffous des Glaçes.

PLANCHE LXXIV.

Deux autres deffeins de Cadres pour des pareilles Tables.

PLANCHE LXXV.

Deux autres deffeins du même genre, lefquels exécutés par un habile fculpteur, feront de la plus grande élégançe.

PLANCHE LXXVI.

Huit deffeins de Confoles en Corniche pour placer des Buftes ou des Bougies.

PLANCHE LXXVII.

Huit deffeins de Bordures pour des miroirs Convexes, ou Concaves; les Bordures font un très joli effet dans un appartement bien meublé.

PLANCHE LXXVIII.

Deux deffeins de Bordures pour des Miroirs Ovales.

PLANCHE LXXIX.

Quatre deffeins de Bordures de miroir, dans un gout d'Architecture.

PLANCHE LXXX.

Deux deffeins de Bordures pour des Trumeaux. les Bordures font entourées, et toutes les deux ont eté executées d'après ce deffein, en Or bruni, et elles ont très belle apparençe.

PLANCHE LXXXI.

Deux Deffeins de Bordures pour des Trumeaux dans un goût d'Architecture, et entourées de glaces.

PLANCHE

(11)

PLATE LXXXII.

A Defign for an elegant Pier Glafs Frame, with Borders ; a Slab Table under ditto.

PLATE LXXXIII.

Three Defigns of Glaffes to line the Piers of Bow-Windows, which have a very good Effect.

PLATE LXXXIV.

Four Defigns of Chimney Glaffes and Pictures over them.

PLATE LXXXV.

Two Defigns for Chimney-pieces, with a Stove Grate.

PLATE LXXXVI.

Two other Defigns of Chimney-pieces, and a pair of Doggs for burning Wood.

PLATE LXXXVII.

Another Defign for a Chimney-piece, with a Stove Grate.

PLATE LXXXVIII.

Nine Defigns of Picture Frames, the Ornaments of which may be extended to fuit any fiz'd Picture.

PLATE LXXXIX.

Two Defigns of Venetian or Philadelphia Stoves, which have been work'd from the Plate, the bright work engraved is laid on black Japan'd Plates; they are very ufeful in preventing Smoak.

PLATES XC, XCI, XCII, XCIII, XCIV, and XCV.

Are Defigns for Stove Grates, Fenders, Dogs, Bracket Irons, Hand Railing, &c.

FINIS.

PLANCHE LXXXII.

Deffein d'une pareille Bordure fort élégante. Cette Bordure eft entourée, et au deffous de la glaçe eft une Table de marbre.

PLANCHE LXXXIII.

Trois Deffeins de Glaçes pour plaçer dans les piédroits des fenêtres faillantes, et elles feront un grand effet.

PLANCHE LXXXIV.

Quatre Deffeins de Glaçes de cheminée avec des Tableaux au deffus.

PLANCHE LXXXV.

Deux Deffeins de manteaux de cheminée, avec une grille à faire du feu.

PLANCHE LXXXVI.

Deux autres Deffeins de manteaux de cheminée, et d'une paire de chenêts, pour bruler du bois.

PLANCHE LXXXVII.

Autre Deffein d'un Manteau de cheminée, avec une grille à faire du feu.

PLANCHE LXXXVIII.

Neuf Deffeins de Bordures de Tableaux, dont les ornemens peuvent s'adapter à des tableaux de toutes grandeurs.

PLANCHE LXXXIX.

Deux Deffeins de Poéles à la Venitienne ou Poéles de Philadelphie, qui ont eté exécutés d'après cette planche. L'ouvrage brillant exprimé dans la gravûre etoit travaillè fur des lames verniffées en noir. Les Poéles font fort utiles pour empêcher la fumée.

Les PLANCHES XC, XCI, XCII, XCIII, XCIV, & XCV.

Sont des Deffeins, de Grilles à faire du feu, de Garde-feux, chenêts, Garde-cendres, Confoles de fer, Rampes, &c.

FIN.

Plate I.

Ornaments for Practice

W.m Ince inv.t et delin.t   Darly sculp.

Plate II.

A Systimatical Order of Raffle Leaf. from the Line of Beauty.

W.ᵗ Ince invᵗ et delin.

Mᴰarly sculp.

Plate III.

Raffle Leaf

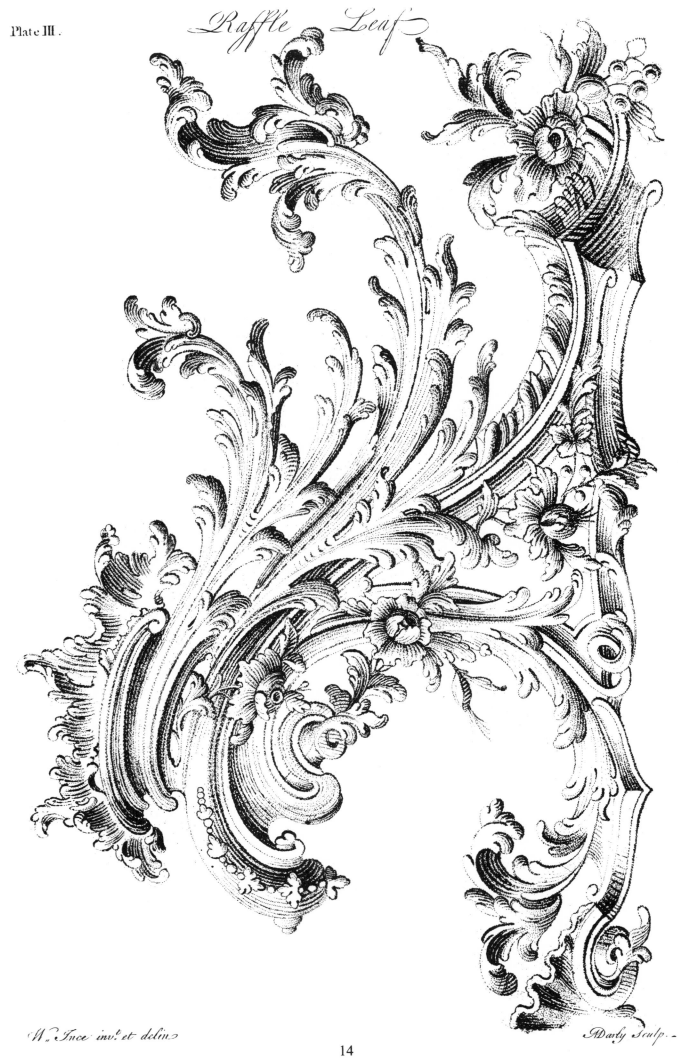

W. Ince inv.t et delin

Darly Sculp.

Plate III.

Hall Chairs.

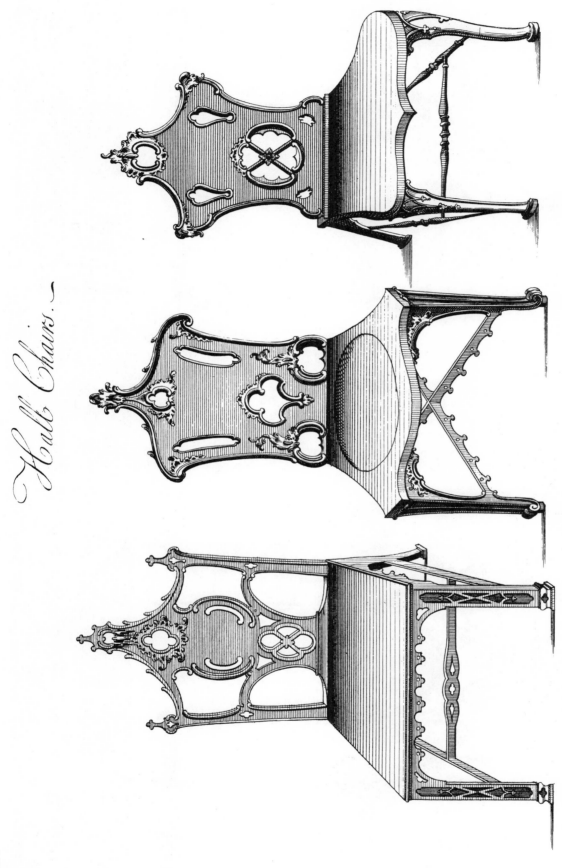

W. Ince inv.t et del.

15

Plate V.

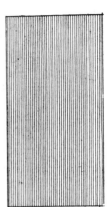

Lanthorns.

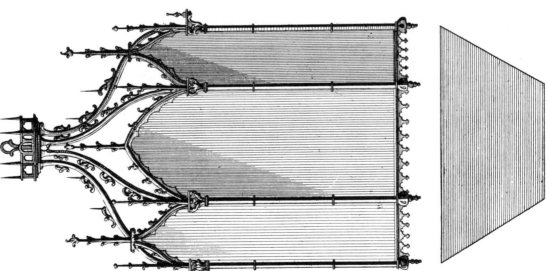

M.ʳ Darly Sculp.

M.ʳ Ince invᵗ et del.

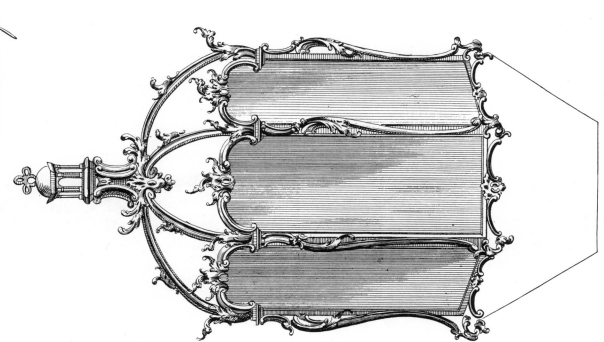

Lanthorns for Wood or Brass.

Plate VI.

Darly Sculp.

M.r Ince inv.t et delin.

Staircase Lights.

Darly sculp.

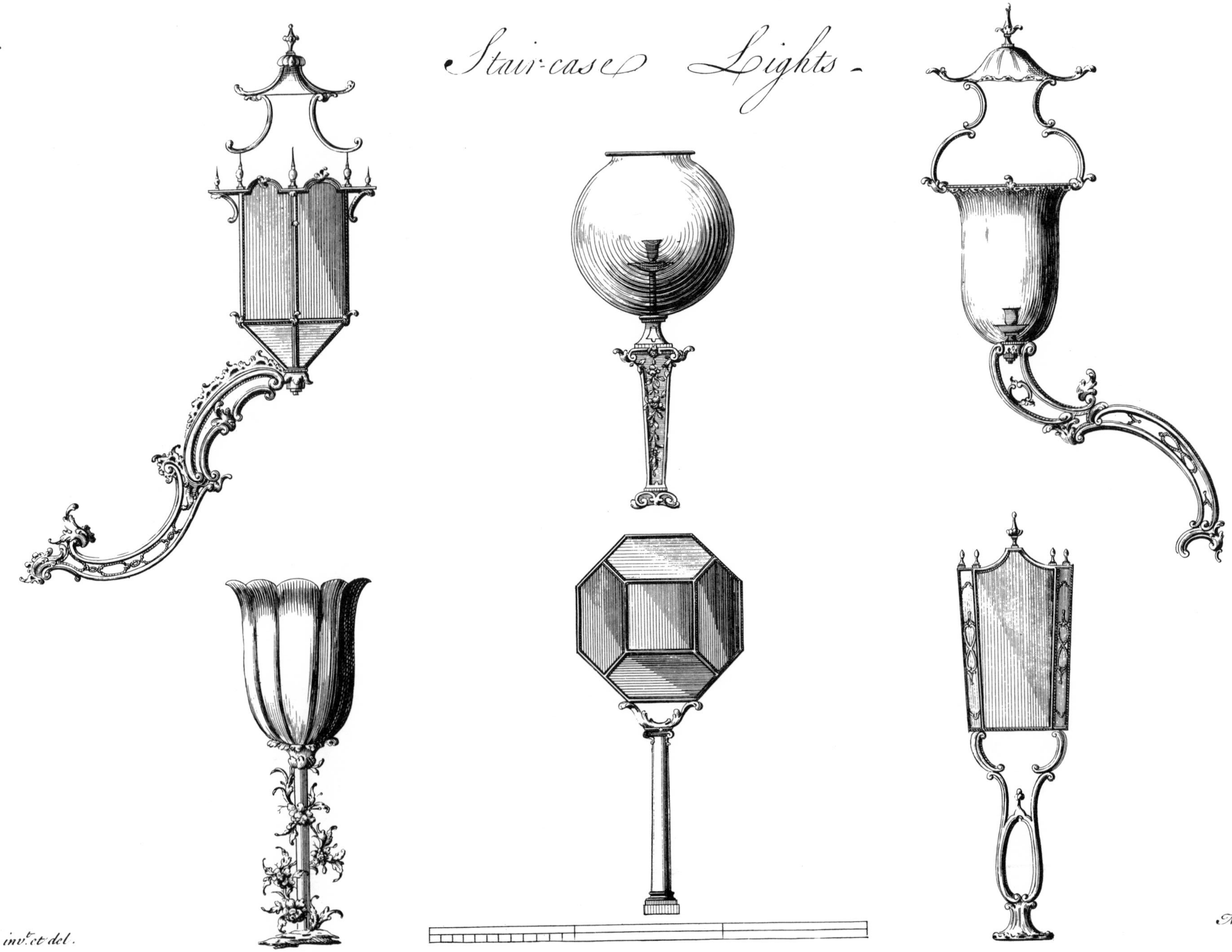

M.ᵃ Ince inv.ᵗ et del.

Plate VII.

18

Plate VIII.

Therms for Busts or Lamps.

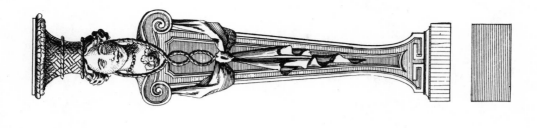

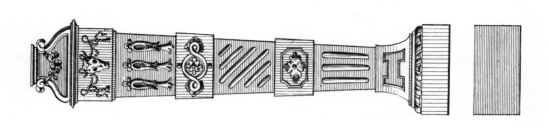

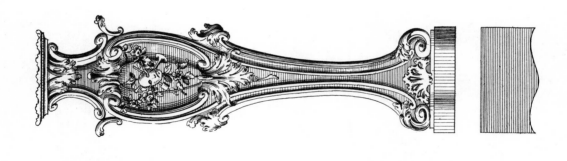

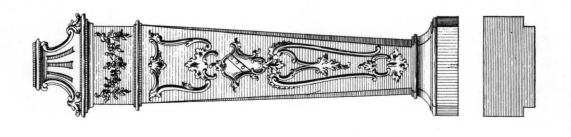

Darly sculp.

Mathew inv:t et delin?

Plate IX.

Parlour Chairs.

M. Ince invt et delin.

20

M Darly sculp.

Plate X.

Parlour Chairs.

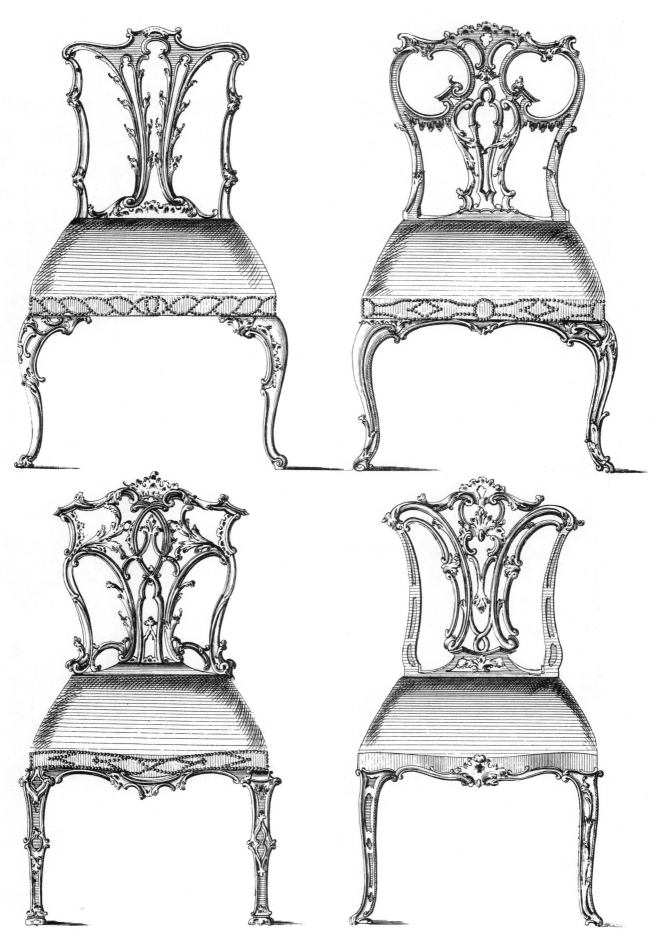

W. Ince inv.t et delin.t

J. Darly sculp.

Plate XI.

Side Board Tables.

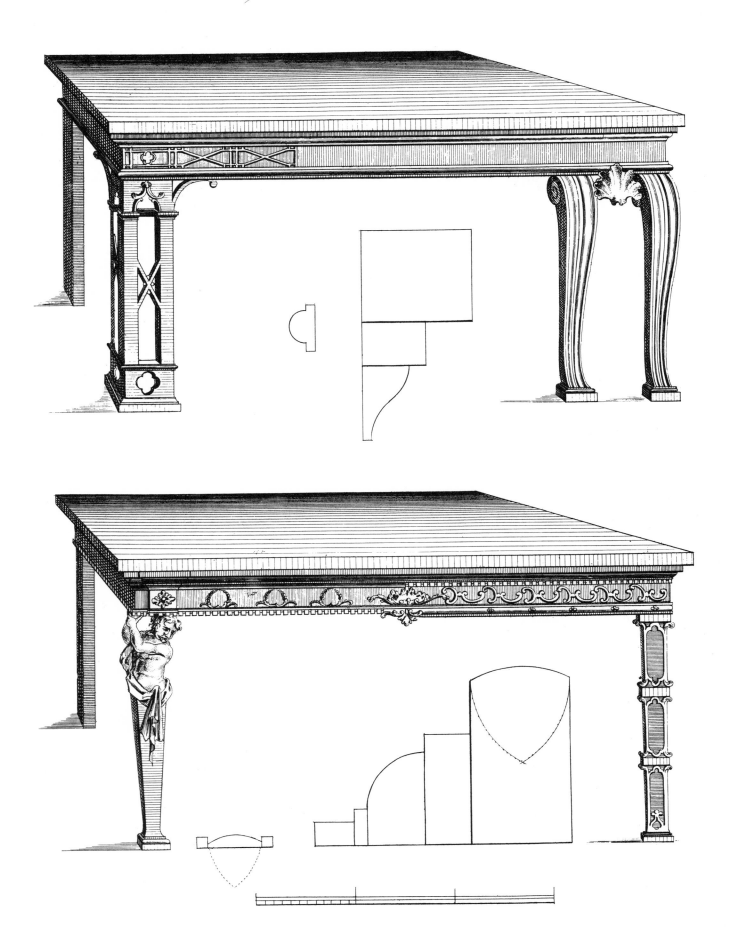

W. Ince inv.t et delin.

M Darly sculp.

Plate. XII.

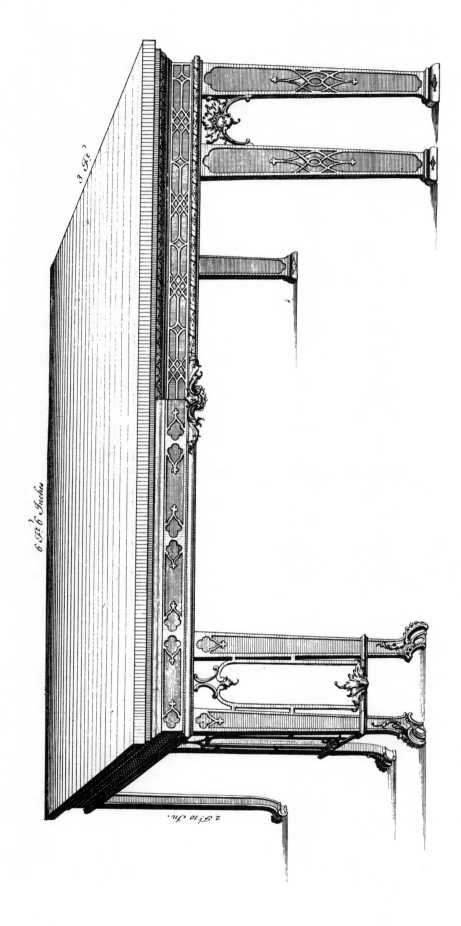

Side Board Table.

6 Ft 6 Inches

3 Ft

2 Ft 10 In.

M.ª Ince inv: et del:

Darly sculp.

Plate XIII.

Claw Tables.—

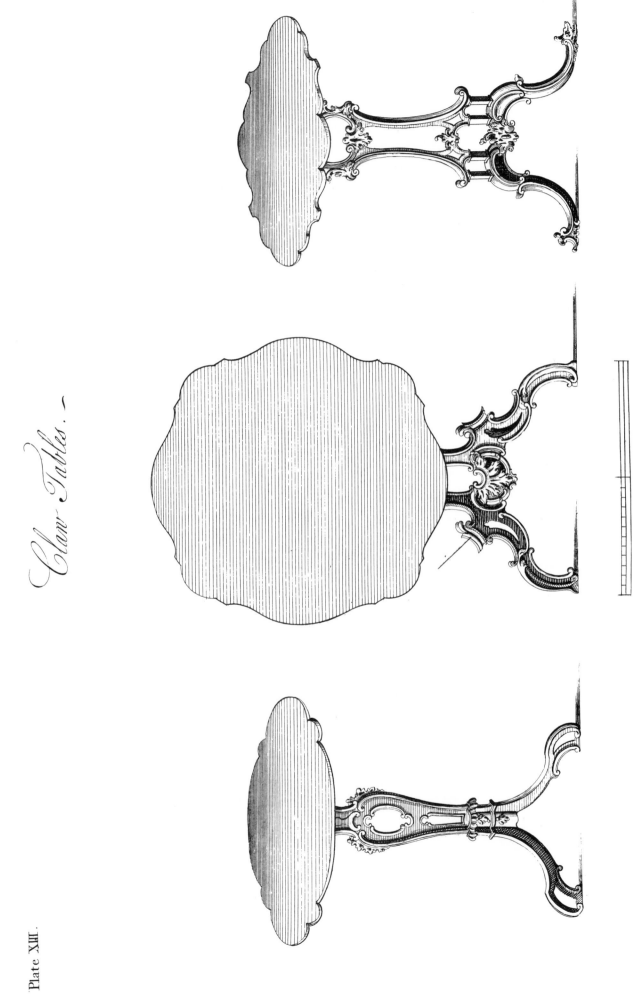

A Darly sculp.—

H. Ince inv.t et del.

24

Plate XIV.

Tea Kettle Stands.

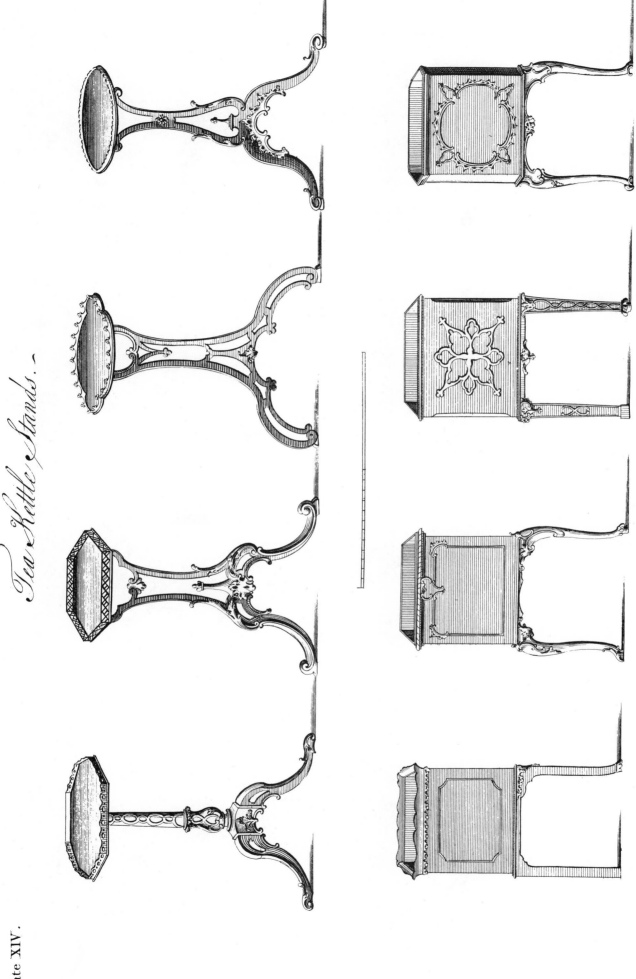

M. Ince inv.t et del.

Darly sculp.

25

Plate XV.

Voiders.

W. Ince inv.t et del.

Darly sculp.

Plate XVI.

Desk & Book Case

M. Ince inv.t et del:

M Darly sculp.

Plate XVII.

Desk & Book Case.

W.ᵐ Ince inv.ᵗ et delin.

M Darly sculp.

Plate XVIII.

Lady's Secretary's.

W. Ince invt. et del.

Marly sculp.

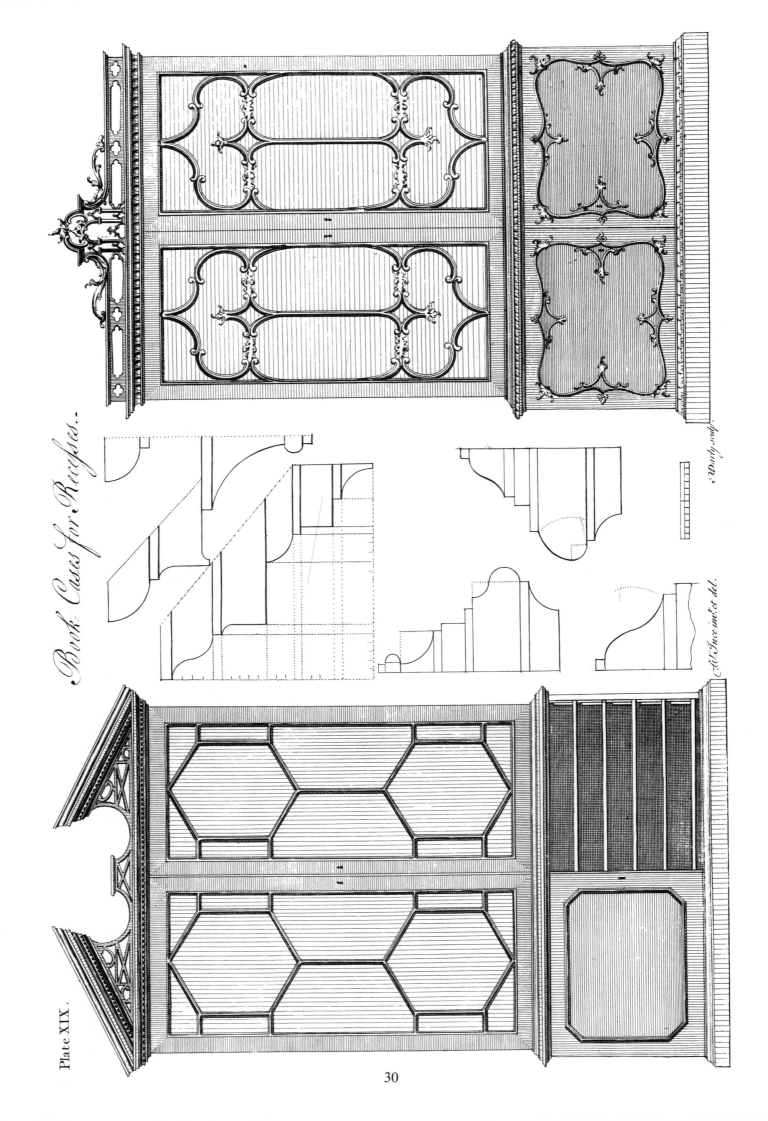

Book Cases for Recejtes.

Plate XIX.

A Ince inv.et del.

W Darly sculp.

30

Plate XX.

Library Bookcase.

Wm Ince inv.t et delin.

I. Darly sculp.

Plate XXI.

Gentlemans Repository

Wm Ince inv.^t et del.

Darly sculp.

Library Steps.

Plate XXII.

F

E

3 ft 1 In.

2 ft 9 In.

1 ft

5 ft 8 In.

2 ft 6 In.

2 ft 8½ In.

4 ft 9 In.

8 In. 6

2 ft.

A

A

A

A. Knee inv.ᵗ & delin.

J. Darly sculp.

Plate XXIII.

Library Tables.

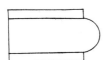

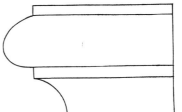

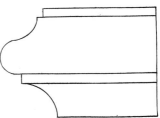

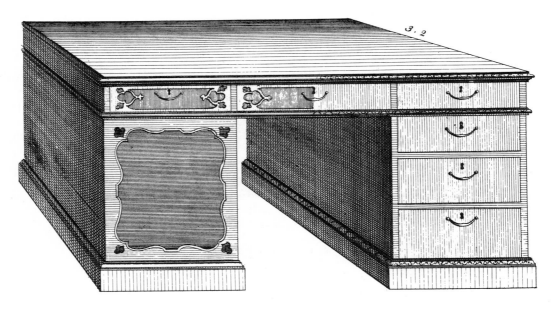

3.2

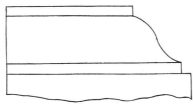

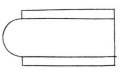

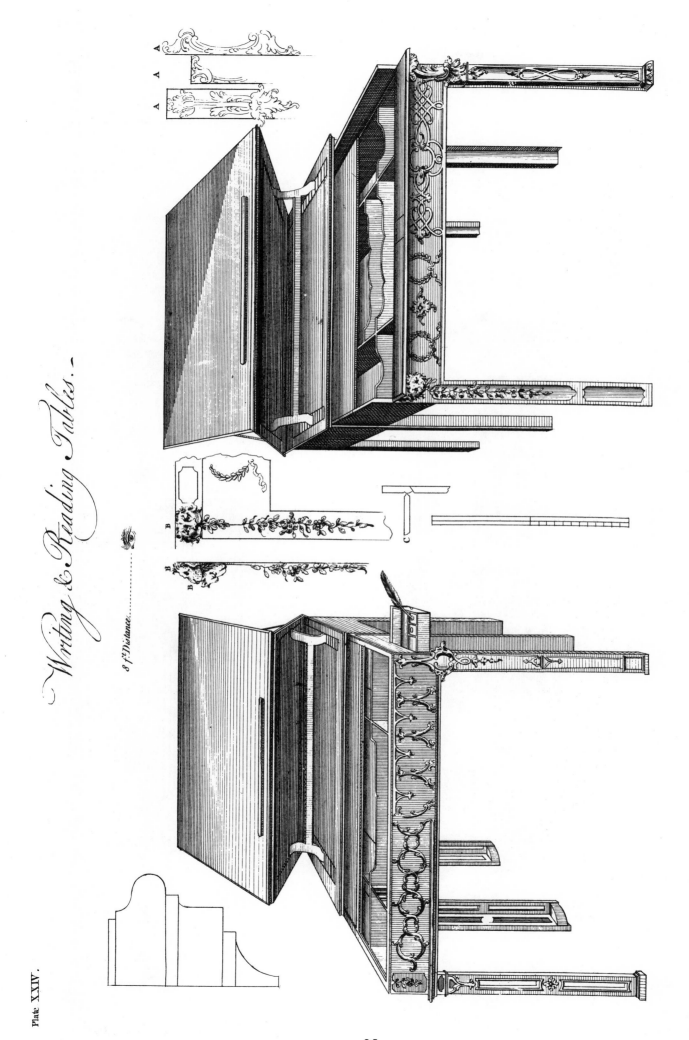

Plate XXIV.

Writing & Reading Tables.

Plate XXV.

Study Table

M. Inir invt et del.

Darly sculp.

36

Plate XXVI.

Reading, or Music Desks.

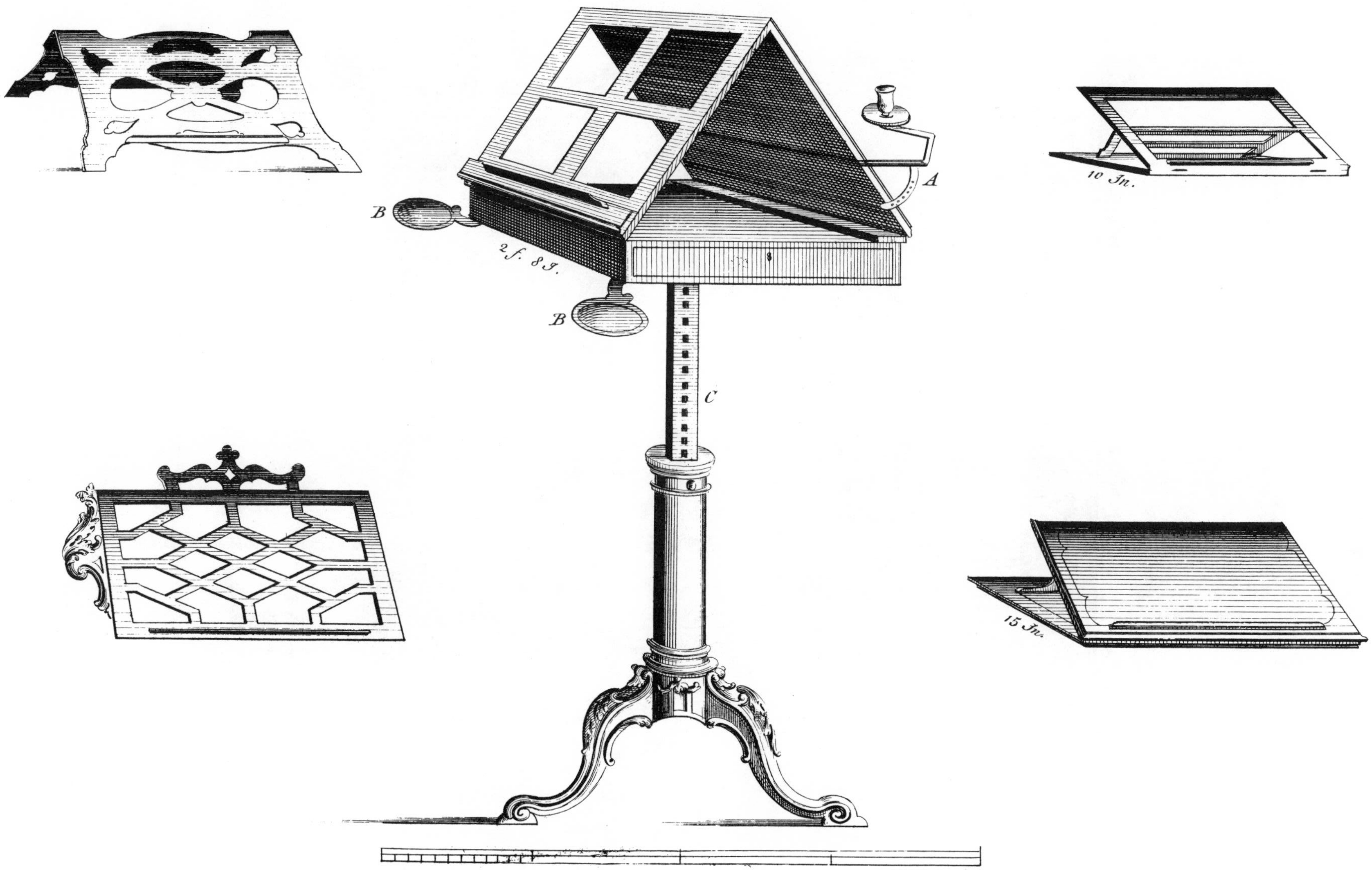

10 In.

15 In.

A

2 f. 85.

B

B

c

M. Ince invt. et delin

Darly sculp.

Plate XXVII.

A Sofa Bed

W. Ince inv.t et delin.

Darly Sculp.t

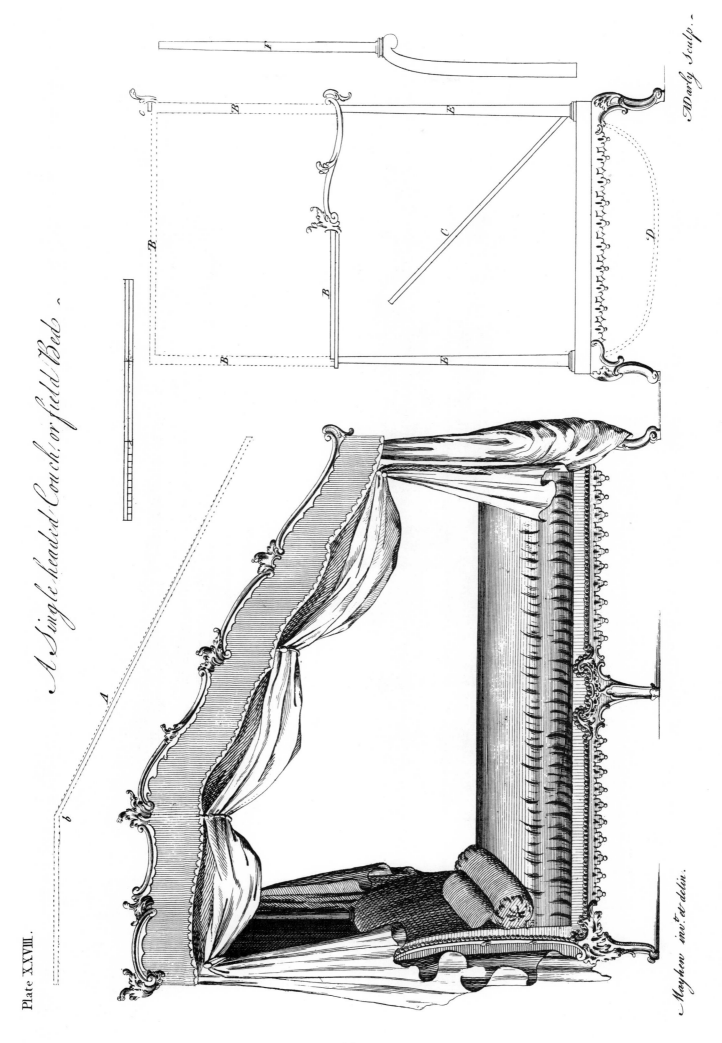

Plate XXVIII.

A Single headed Couch, or field Bed.

T Darly Sculp.

Mayhew inv.t et delin.

39

Plate XXIX.

A Bed.

Mayhew invt et del.

Darly sculp.

Plate XXX.

A Bed for an Alcove

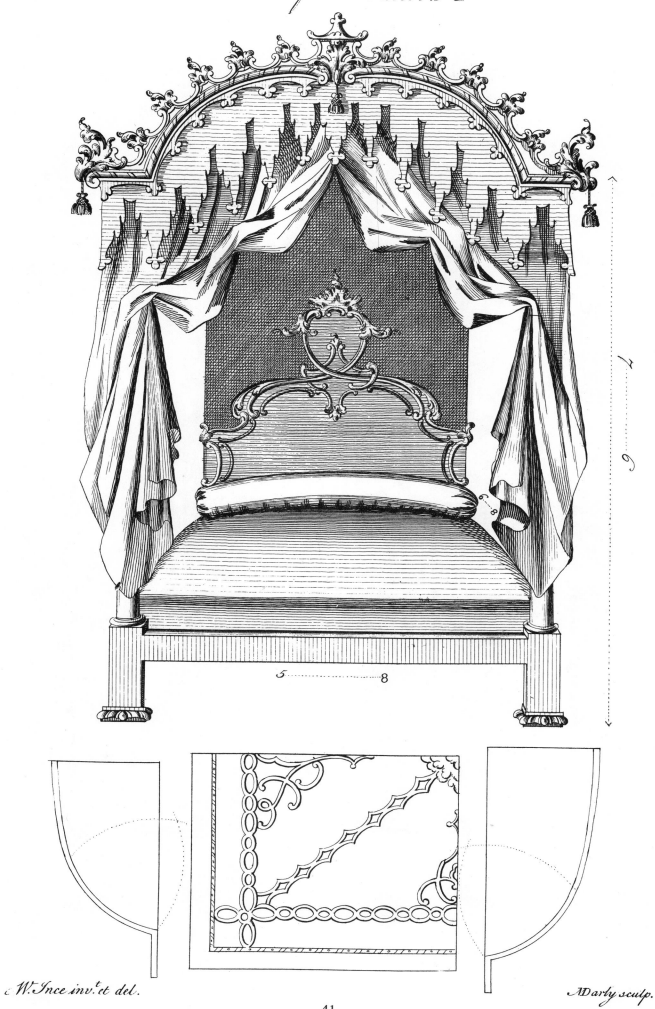

W. Ince inv.t et del.

M. Darly sculp.

Plate XXXI.

French Bed.

Mayhew invt. et del.

Darly sculp.

Plate XXXII.

Dome Bed.

M. Ince inv.t et del.

Darly sculp.

Plate XXXIII.

Night Tables.

W. Ince inv.t et del.

T Darby sculp.

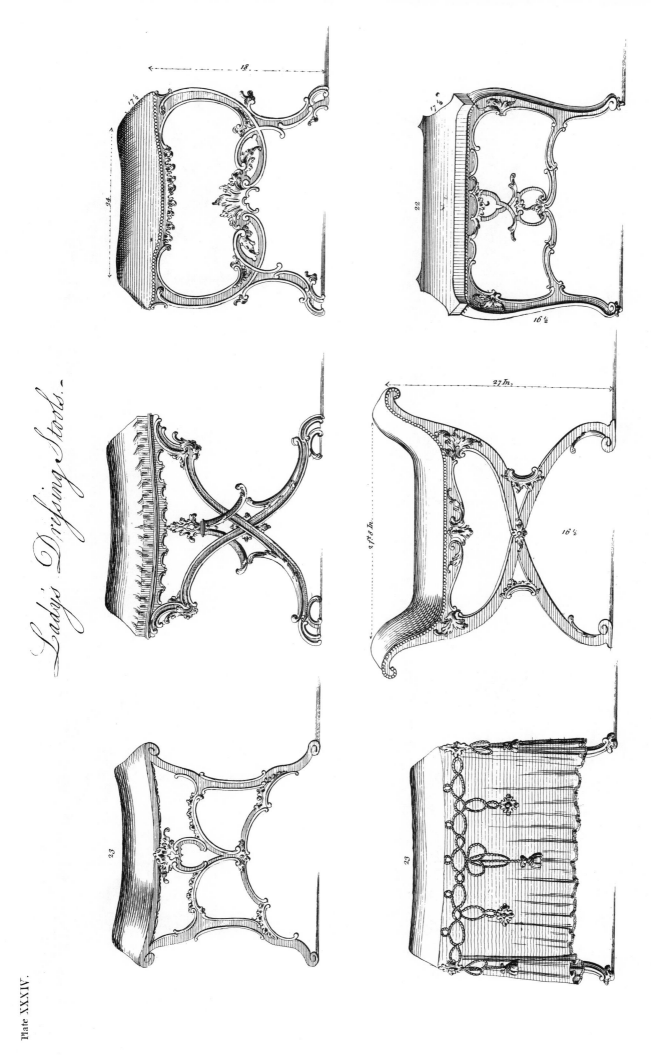

Plate XXXIV.

Lady's Drifsing Stools.

18

17½

24

22

17½

16½

27 In:

4 ft 8 In:

16½

23

23

M. Ince inv.t et delin.

Marly sculp.

45

Plate XXXV.

Dressing Chairs

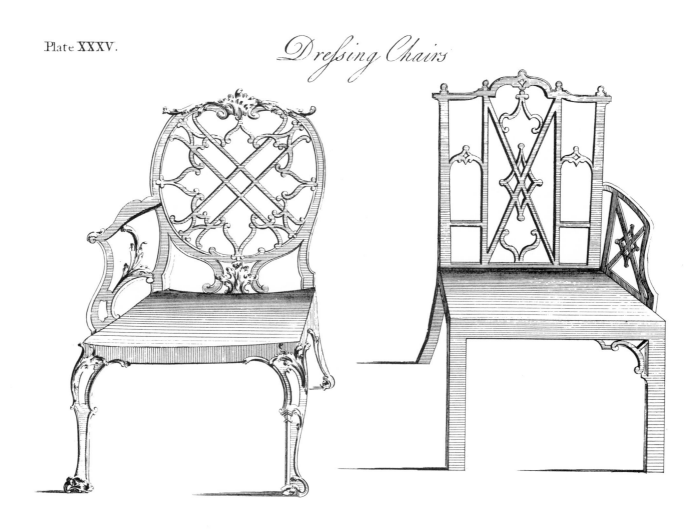

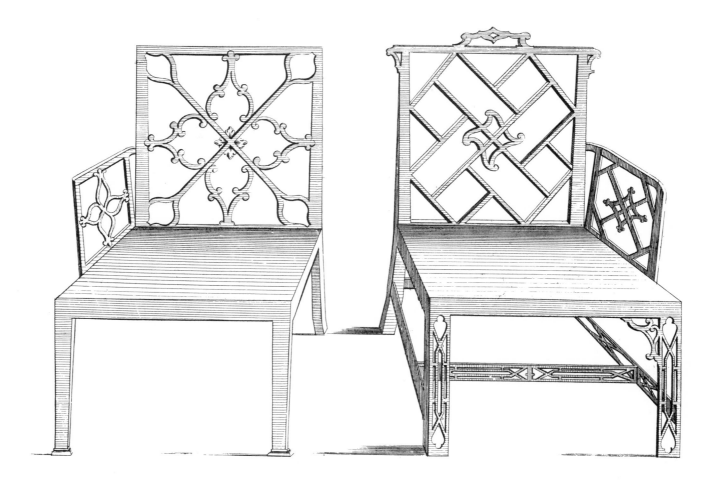

I. Mayhew invᵗ et delinᵗ

Darly Sculp.

Plate XXXVI.

Ladys Toilettas

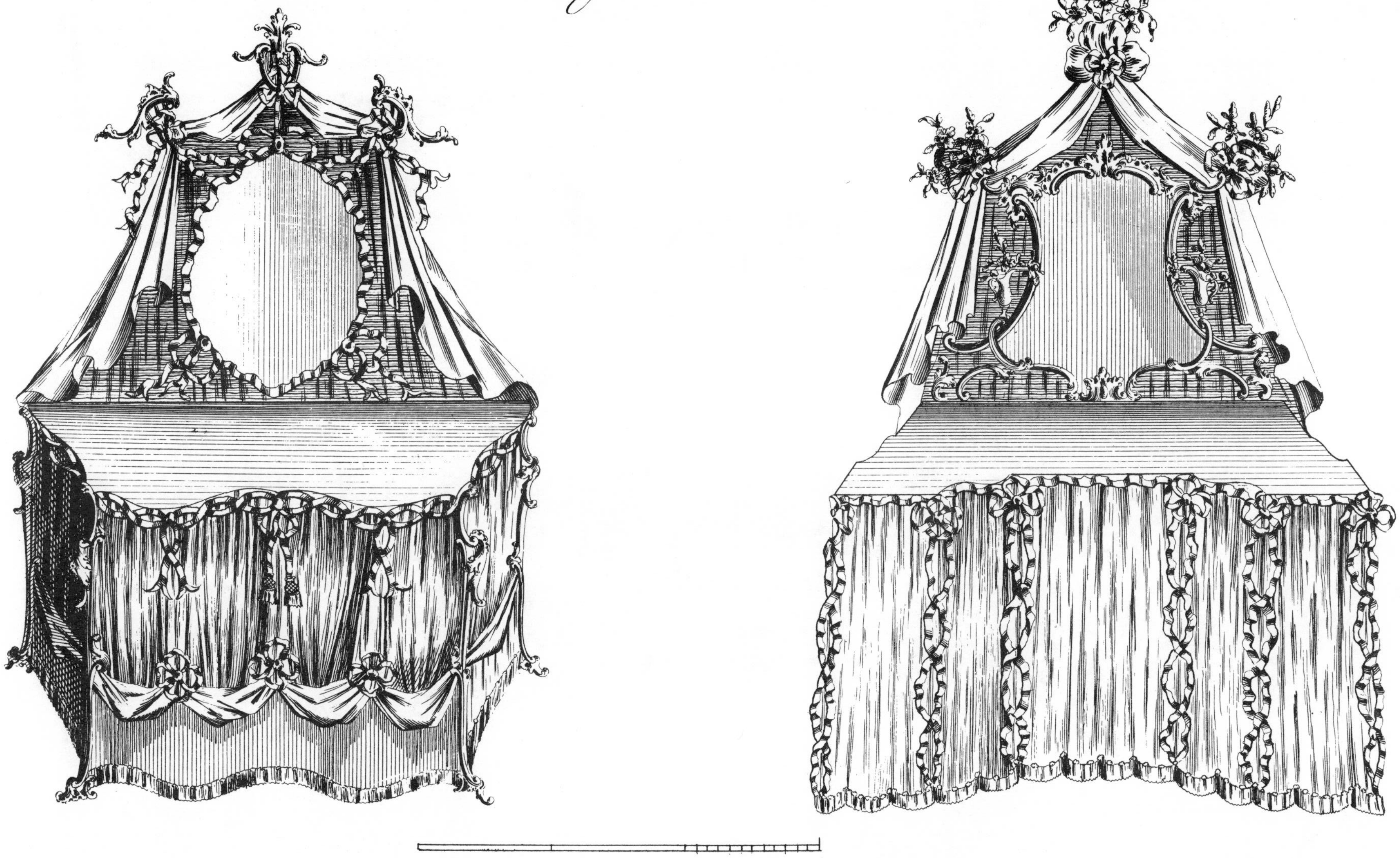

Darly Sculp.

W. Ince inv.t et delin.

Plate XXXVII

A Lady's Toilette.

W. Ince inv.t et del.

Darly sculp.

Plate XXXVIII.

Lady's Dressing Tables.

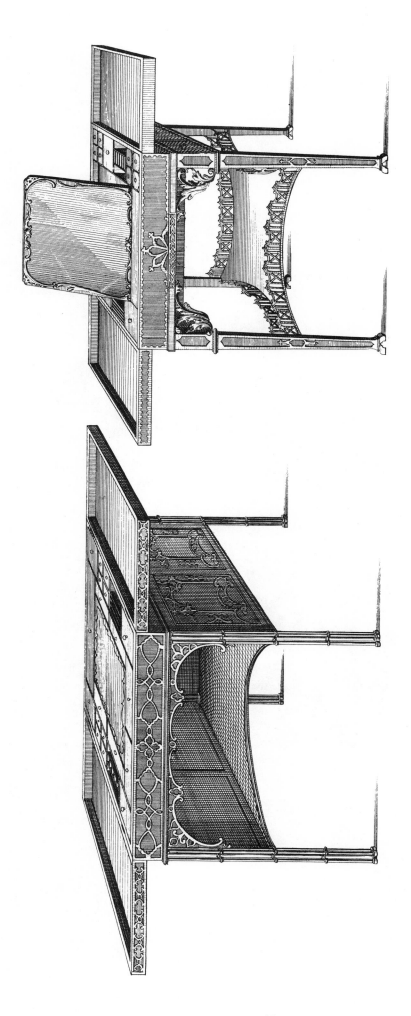

M.^rInce inv.^t et del.

Darly sculp.

Plate XXXIX.

Lady's *Apparatus.*

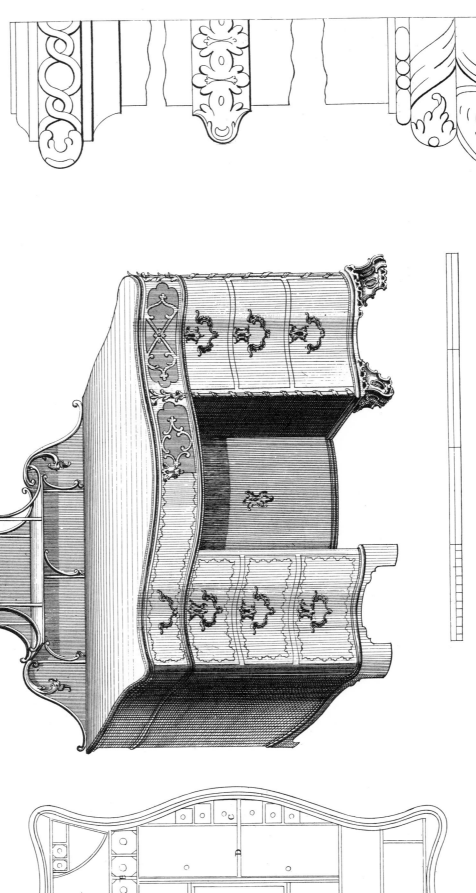

A

C

O

D

E

A. Ince invt et del..

ADarly sculp.

50

Dressing Table

Bureau

Plate. XL.

51

Plate XLI.

Commode *Dressing Tables.*

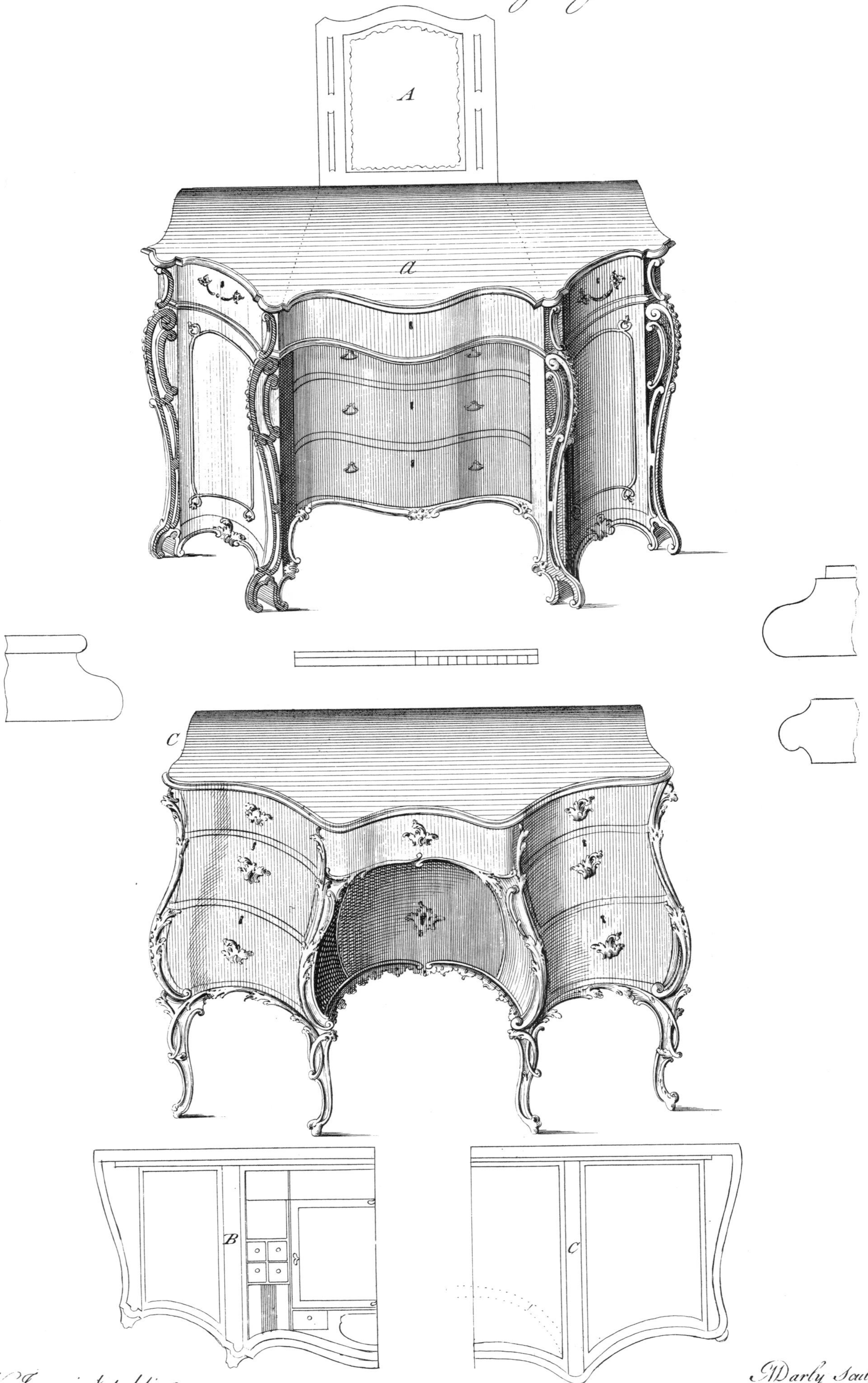

A

a

C

B

C

W. Ince inv.^t et delin

Darly Sculp.

Plate XLII.

Bureau Tables.

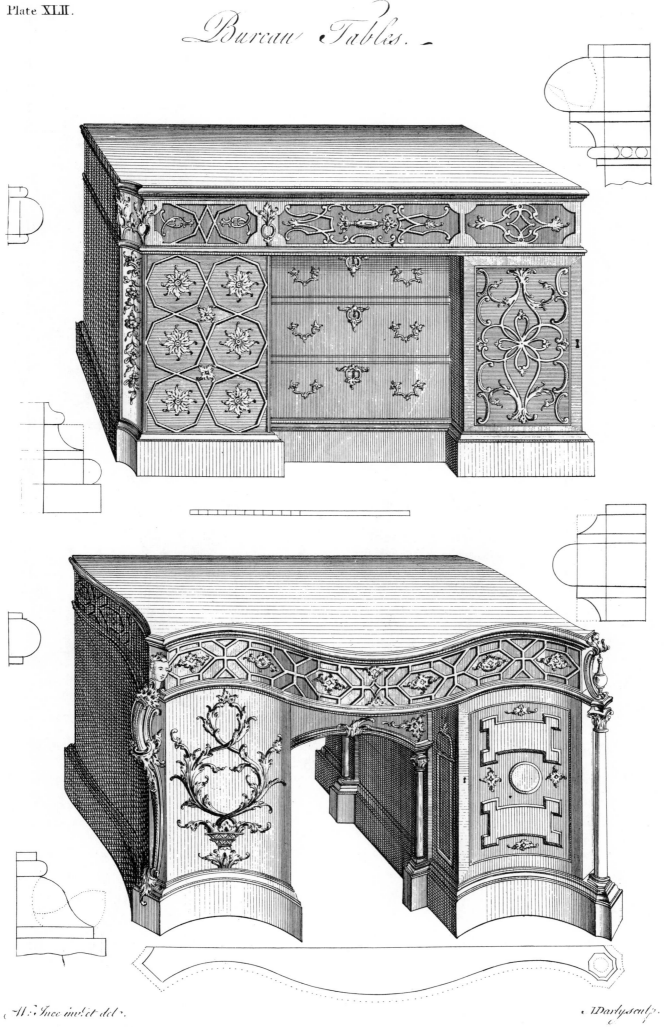

M.ᵉ Ince inv.ᵗ et del.ᵗ   I.Darly sculp.

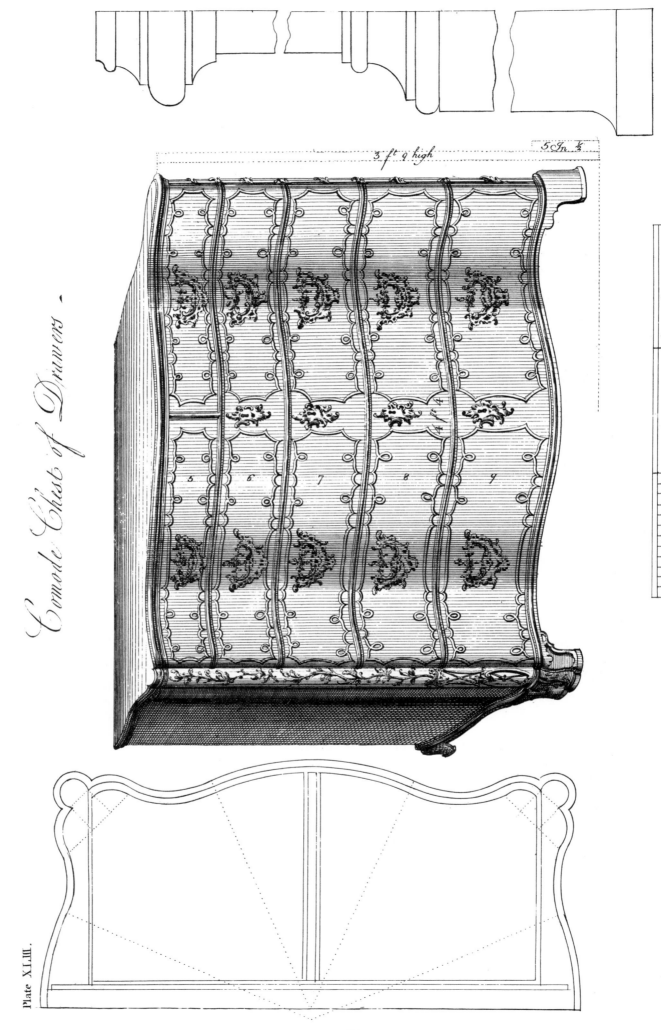

Comode Chest of Drawers.

3 ft 9 high

5 In ⅓

Plate XLIII.

N Darly sculp.

W. Ince invt delin.

Plate XLIV.

Cloaths Chests.

Mᵉ Ince invᵗ et delinᵗ

Darly sculp.

Plate XLV

China Shelves.

Darly sculp.

I. Ince inv.t et del.

56

Plate XLVI.

China Table & Shelf.

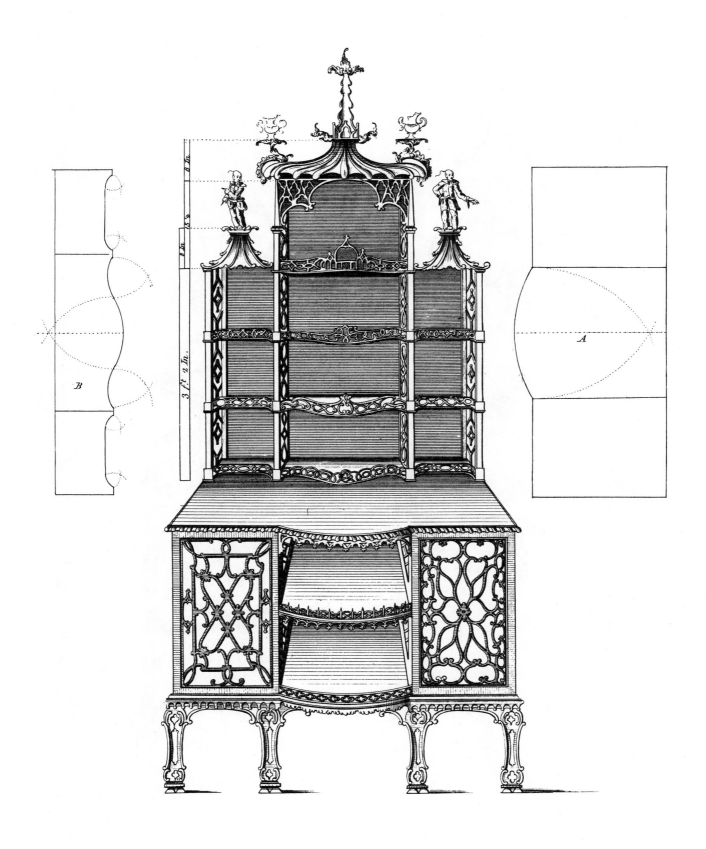

Mayhew inv.t et del.   Darly sculp.

Plate XLVII.

Ecoineurs.

W.m Ince inv.t et delin.

Darly sculp.

Plate XLVIII.

A China Case.

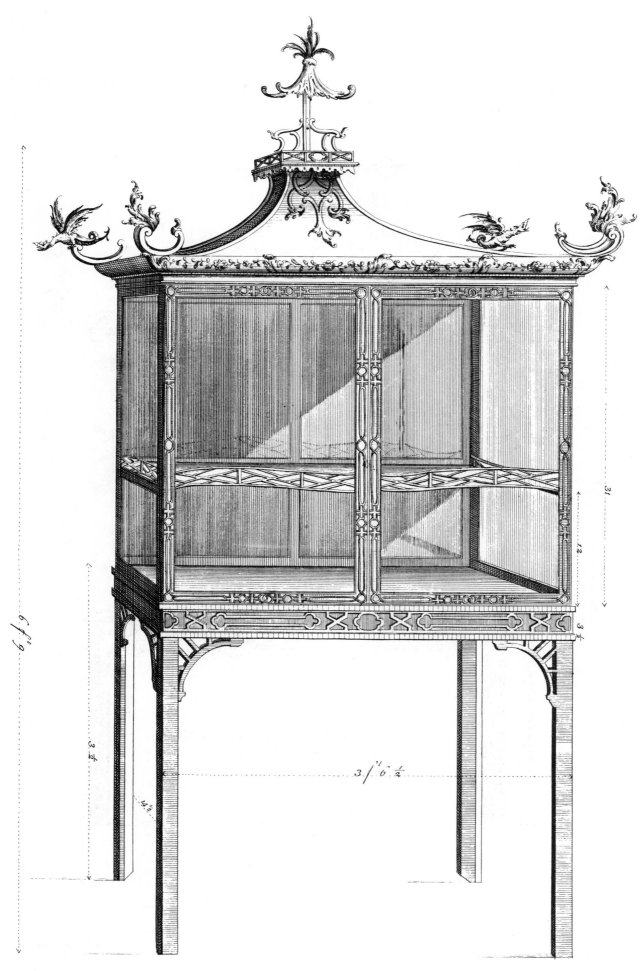

W.ᵐ Ince inv.ᵗ et delin.ᵗ

Darly sculp.

Plate XLIX.

China Case

Wm Ince inv.^t et delin.^t

Darly Sculp.^t

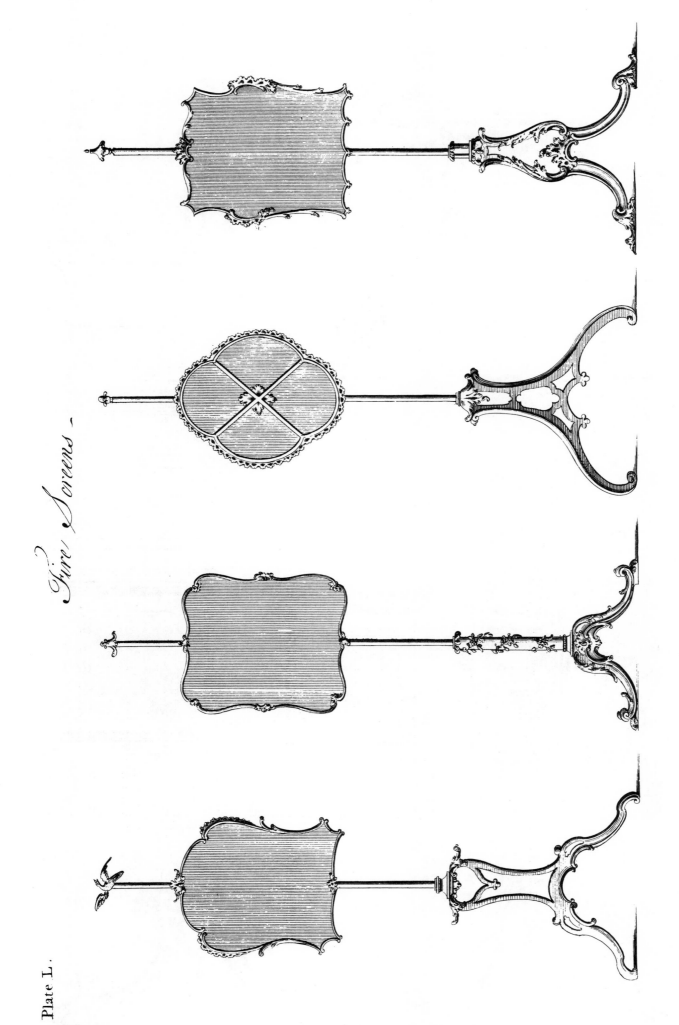

Plate L.

Fire Screens -

W.º Ince inv.t et delin.

ADarly Sculp.

61

Plate LI.

Stands for Figures & China Jars...

M. Ince inv.t et del.

M Darly Sculp.

Plate LII.

7 Feet 6 Inches distance.

Card Tables.

5 f.t 3 In. Sight

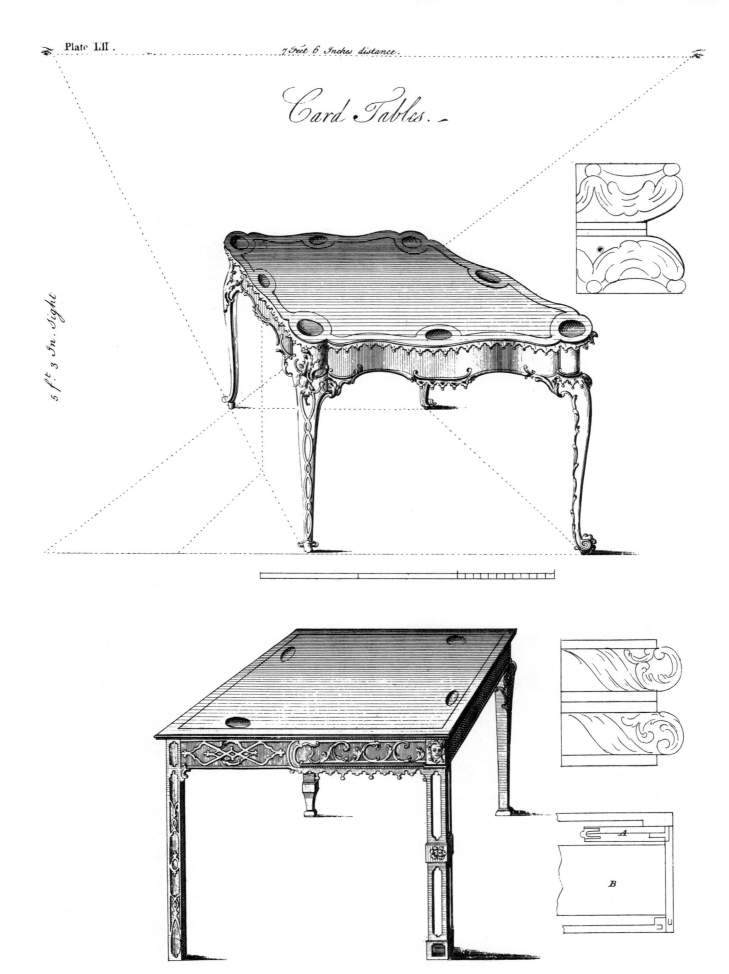

W. Ince inv.t et delin.t

63

. I Darly sculp.

Plate LIII.

Card Tables

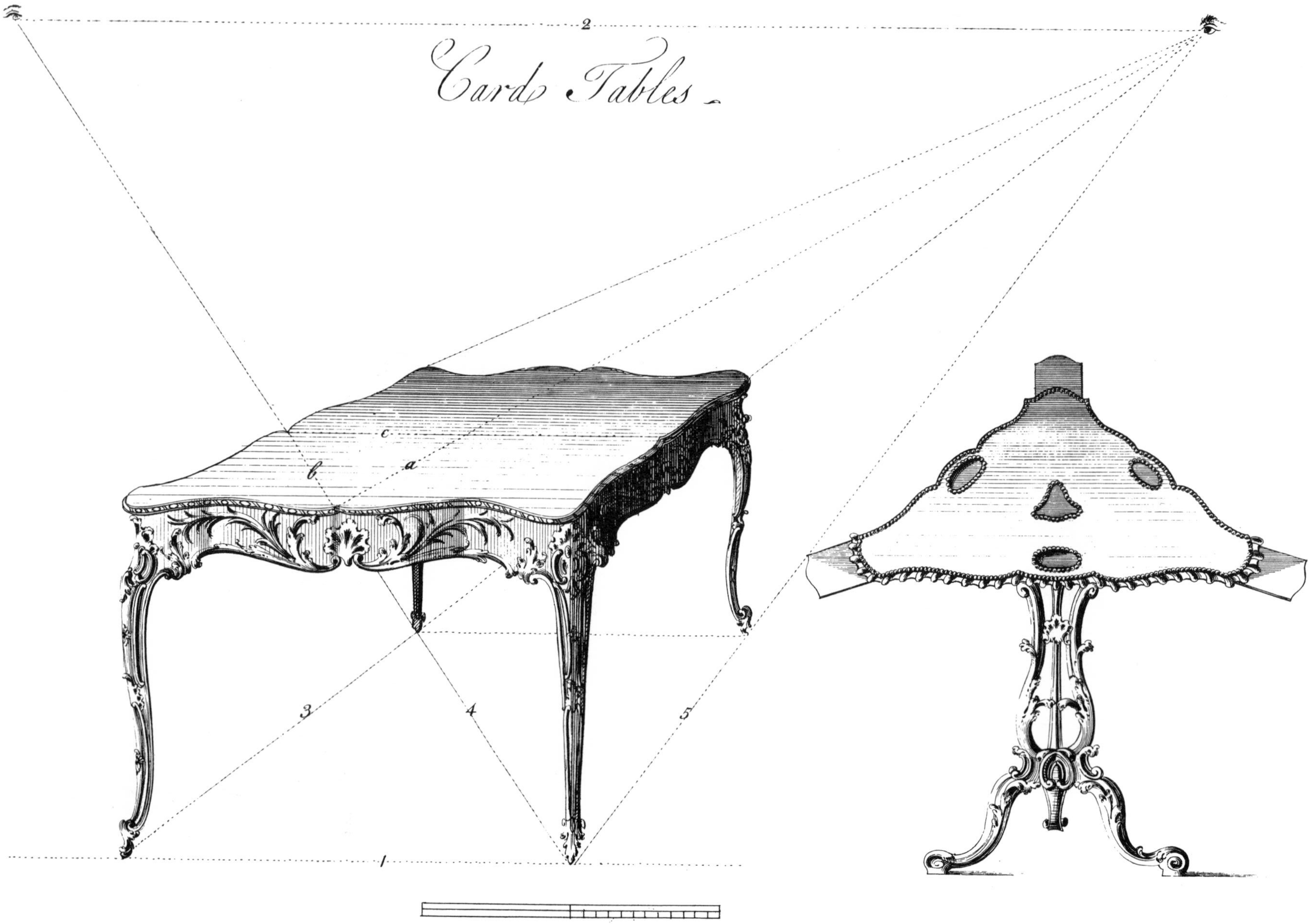

2

5

4

3

b

a

A. Ince inv.t et delin

Darty sculp.t

Plate LIV.

Organ Case.

W. Ince invt. et delt

Darly sculp.

Plate LV.

Back Stools.

M. Ince inv.t et del.t

Darly sculp.

66

Plate LVI.

Back Stools.

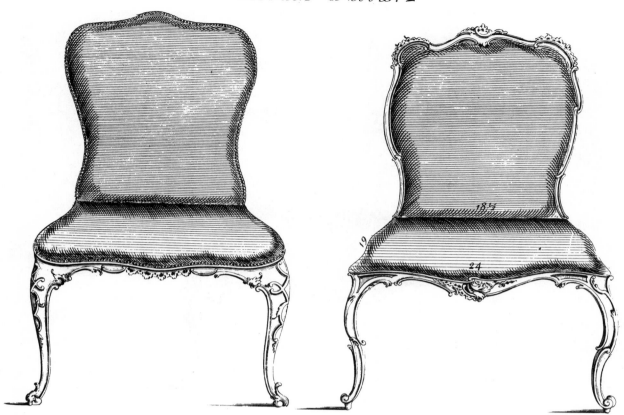

W.ᵉ Ince invᵗ et delin

Darly sculp.

Plate LVII .

French Corner Chairs.

Mayhew invt. et delt.

MDarly sculp

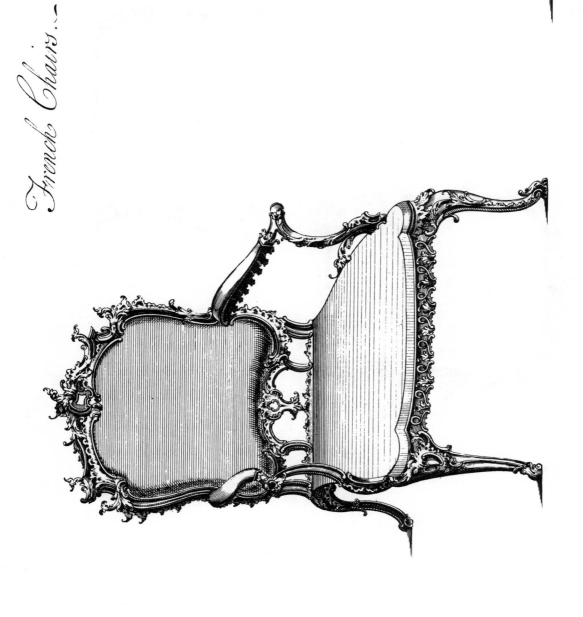

French Chairs.

Plate LVIII.

A.Darly sculp.

M. Ince invt et del.

Plate LIX.

French Chairs.

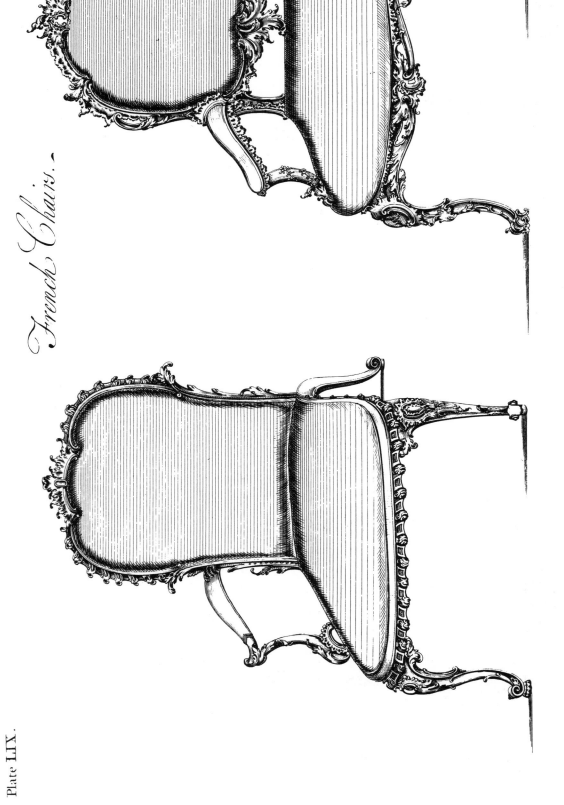

A. Jux invt et delt

JDarly sculp

Plate LX.

Burzairs

Mayhew inv.t et del.

Darly sculp..

Plate LXI.

French Stools

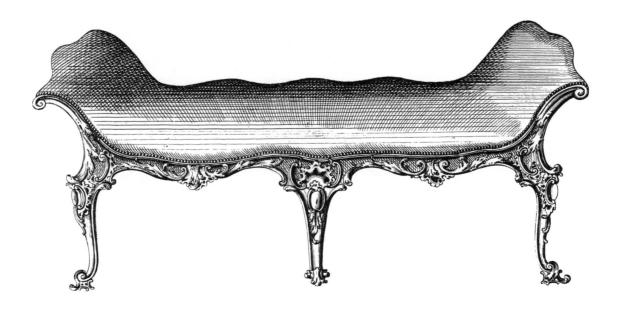

Mayhew inv.t et delin.

A.Darley sculp.

Plate LXII.

Sofas.

Mayhew inv.t et del.

M.Darlysculp

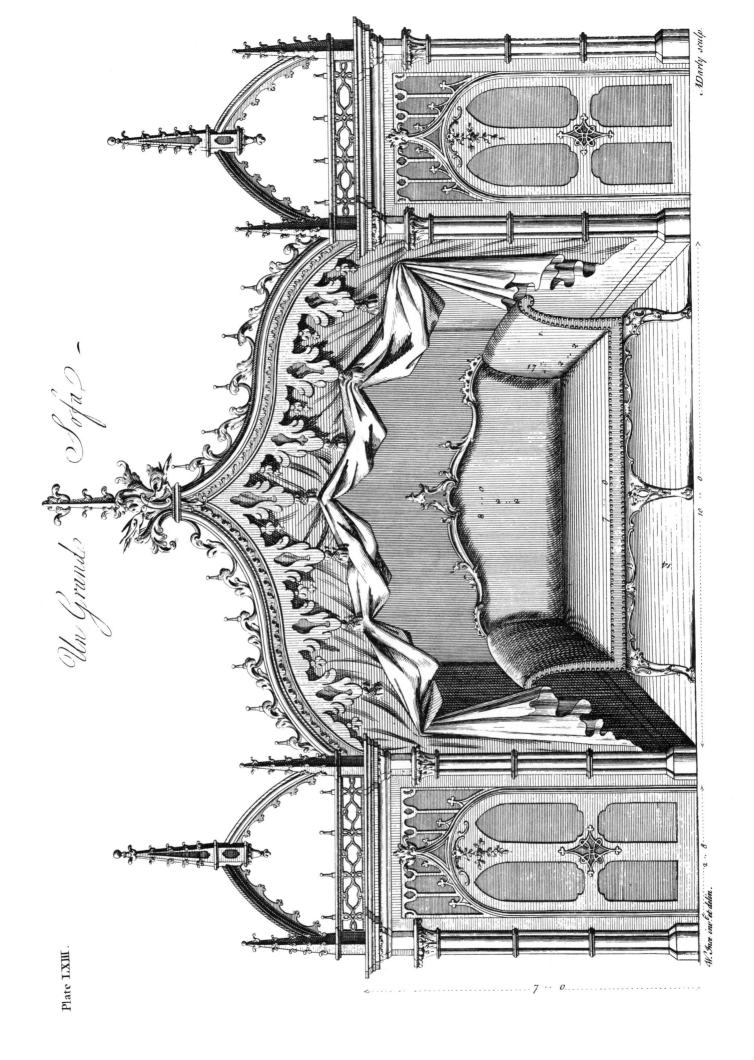

Plate LXIII.

Un Grande Sofa

M. Suie inv. et delin.

A Darly sculp.

74

Plate LXIV.

Couch.

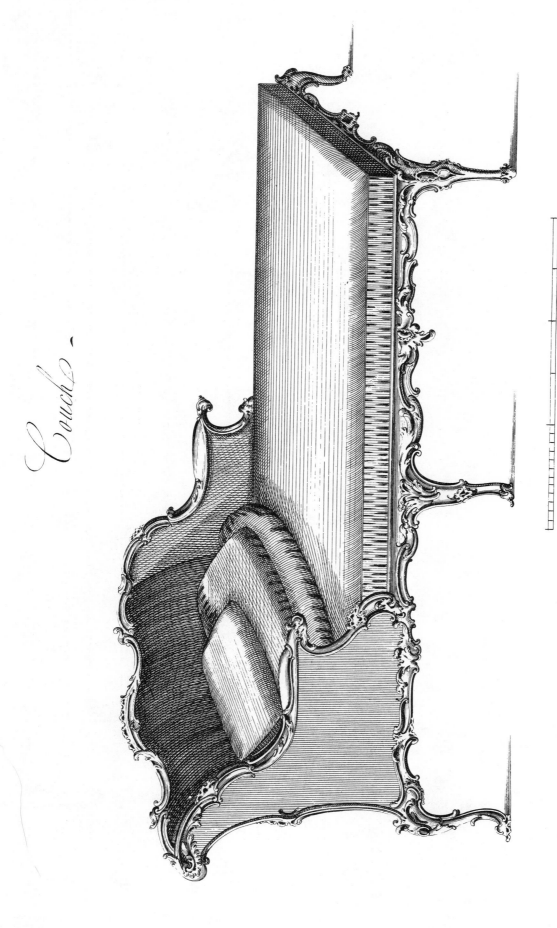

Mayhew inv.t et del.

Darly sculp.

Plate LXV.

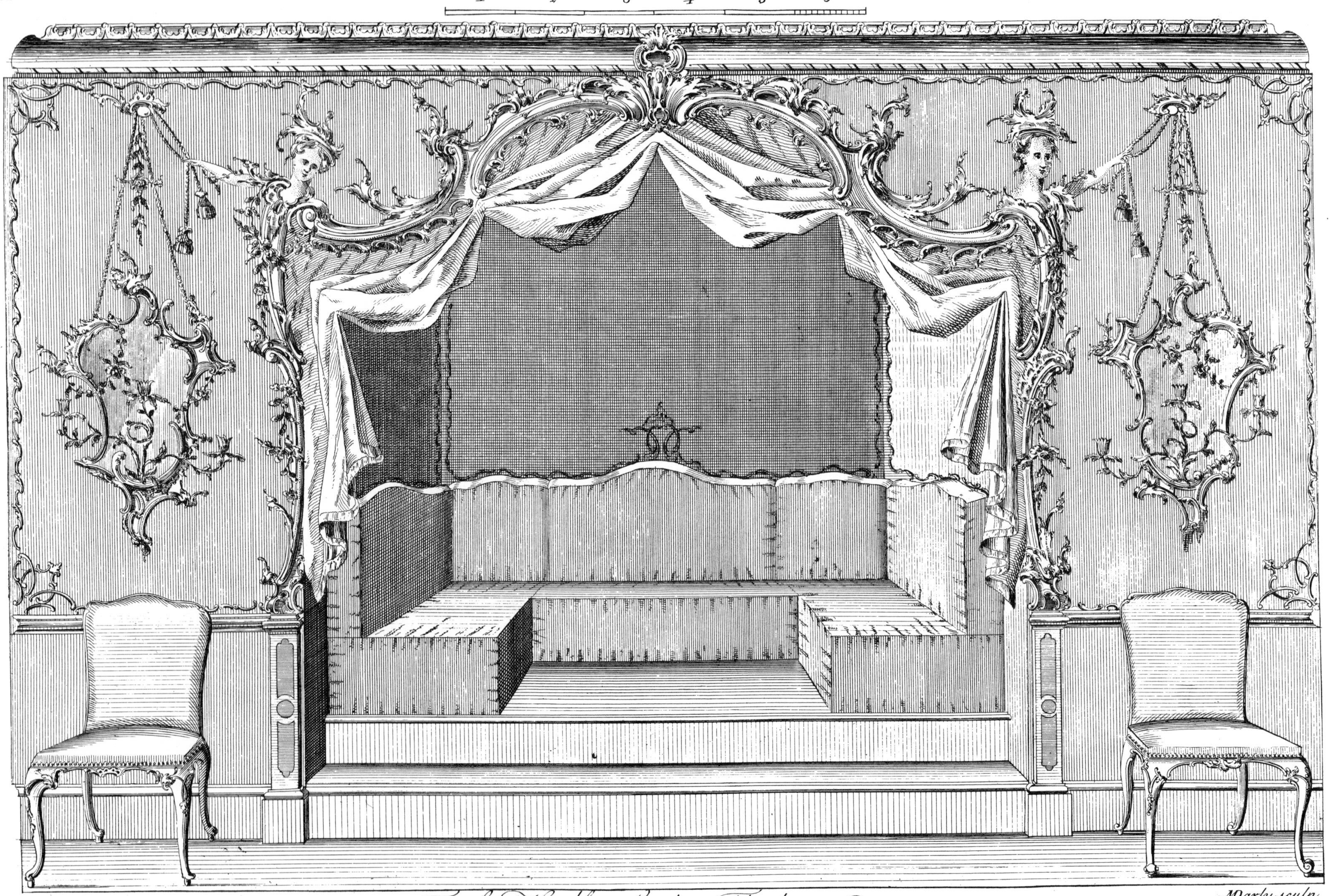

M Darly sculp.

To the Hon.ble Lady Fludyer

This SIDE SECTION of the DRESSING ROOM, is most humbly Inscrib'd by her Ladyships most Obed.t hum.ble Serv.ts J. Mayhew & W. Ince {Inv.ts et Del.ts

Plate LXVI.

A Candlestick.

M.ᵗ Ince invᵗ et delinᵗ.

Darly sculp.

Plate LXVII.

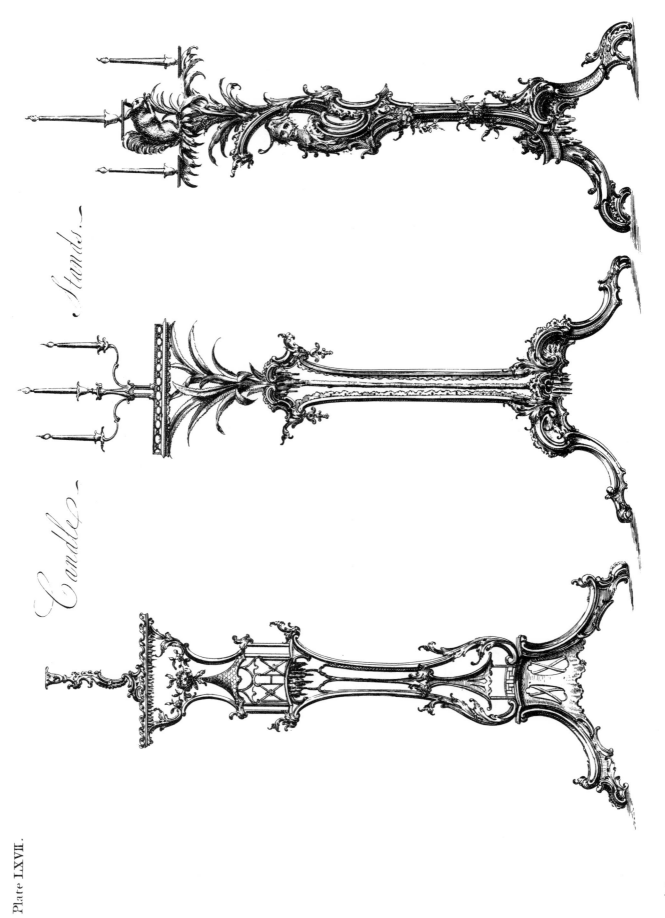

Candle — Stands —

M. Lock inv.t del.

TDarly sculp.

78

Plate LXVIII.

Candle Stands.

M. Ince inv.t et delin.t

Darly Sculp.

79

Plate LXIX.

Candle Stands

Darly Sculp.

W. Ince inv.t et delin.

80

Plate LXX .

Girandolus

Derly Sculp

N. Frex inv.t et delin.t

Plate LXXI.

Darly Sculp.

Illumi. =maries.=

W.ᵐ Ince. inv.ᵗ et delin.

Plate LXXII.

Chandeliers.

W.Ince inv.t et del.
M.Darly sculp.

83

Plate LXXIII.

Slab Frames.

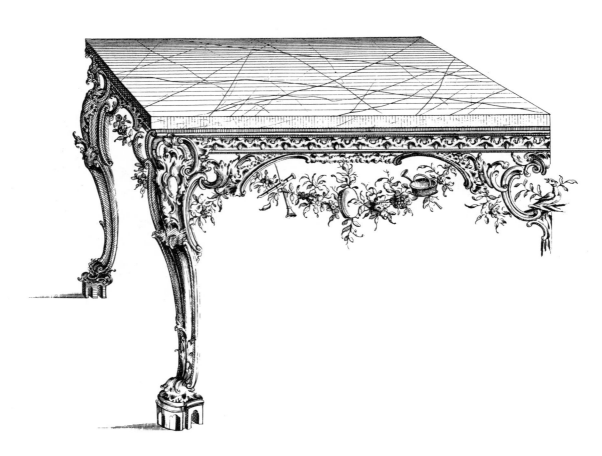

H. Ince invᵗ et del.

Darly sculp.

Plate LXXIV.

Slab Frames.

W.ᵐ Ince invᵗ et del.

M.Darly sculp.

Plate LXXV.

Tables for Slabs.

W. Ince invt et delin.

Darly sculp.

Darly Sculp.ᵗ

Brackets

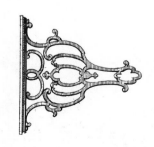

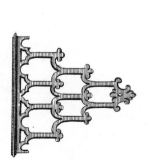

Plate LXXVI.

W.ᵐ Ince inv.ᵗ et delin.

Frames for Convex or Concave Glasses.

W. Darly sculp.

M. Ince inv. et delin.

Plate LXXVII

Plate LXXVIII.

Oval Glass-frames. —

W.ᵗ Ince invᵗ et del.

M.Darly sculp.

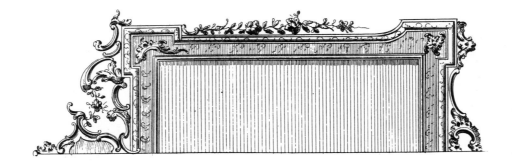

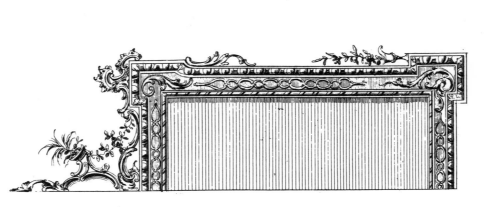

Plate LXXIX.

Architectural Frames.

T. Darly sculp.—

W.ᵐ Ince inv.ᵗ et del.

Plate LXXX.

Pier Glasses.

W.ᵐ Ince inv.ᵗ et delin.

Marly sculp.

Plate LXXXI.

Architectural   Pier Glasses.

Me Ince inv. et delin.   M. Darly sculp.

Plate LXXXII.

Pier Glass & Table.

W. Ince inv.t et del.

I. Darly sculp.

Plate LXXXIII.

Glass's for the Piers in Bow Windows.

1   2   3

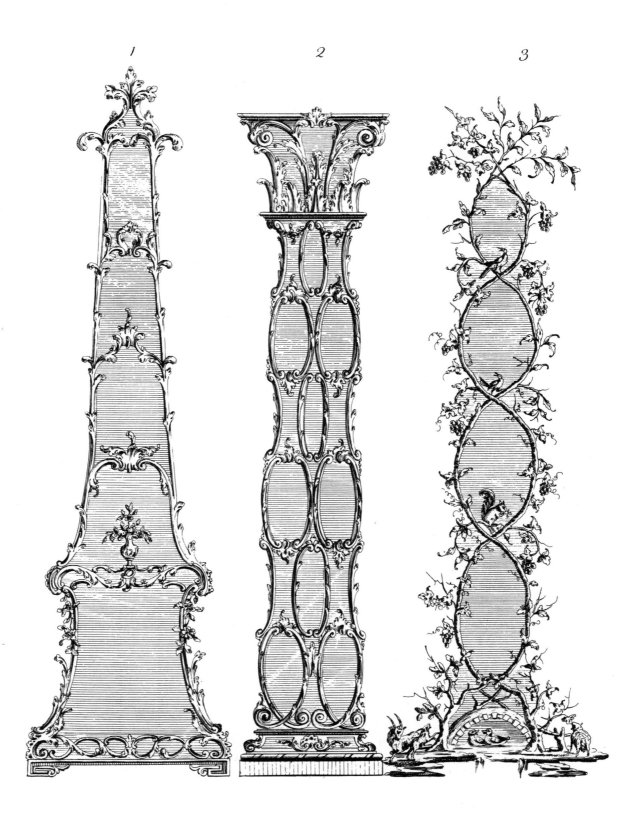

W. Ince invt et delin   Darly sculp

Plate LXXXIV.

Chimney Glass & Picture Frames.

H.Inwwinck. et del.

T.Darly.sculp.

Plate LXXXV.

Chimney Pieces &c.

W. Ince inv.t et del

Darly sculp.

Plate LXXXVI.

W. Ince invt et del.

Darly sculp.

Chimney Piece &c.

W. Ince invt. et del.

Darly sculp.

Plate LXXXVII.

Plate LXXXVIII.

Picture Frames.

M: Ince inv.t et delin.

Darly sculp.

Plate LXXXIX.

Venetian Stores.

ADarly sculp.

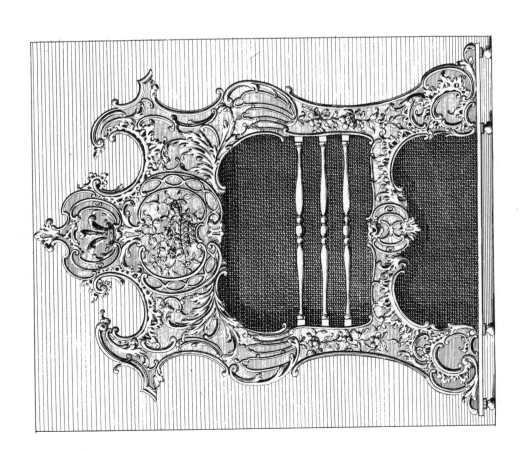

M. Ince inv.t et delin.

Plate 90.

Stove　　　*Grate*

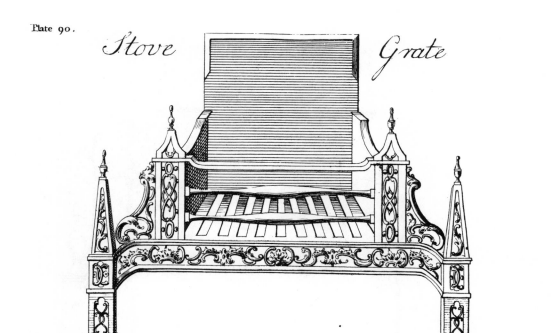

Plate 91.

Stove　　　*Grate*

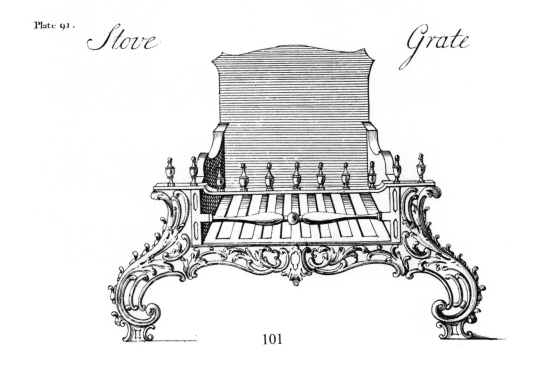

Plate 92.

Stove   *Grate*

Plate 93.

Fenders

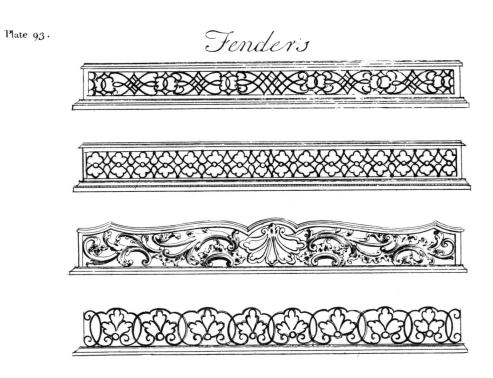

102

Plate 94.

Brachetts for Marble Slabs

Plate 95.

Hand rail for a Belcony

Dogs

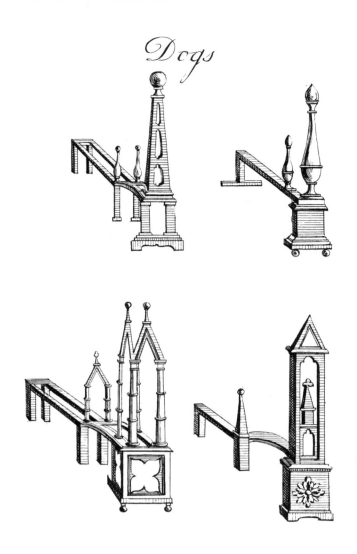

Stair Case *Railing*

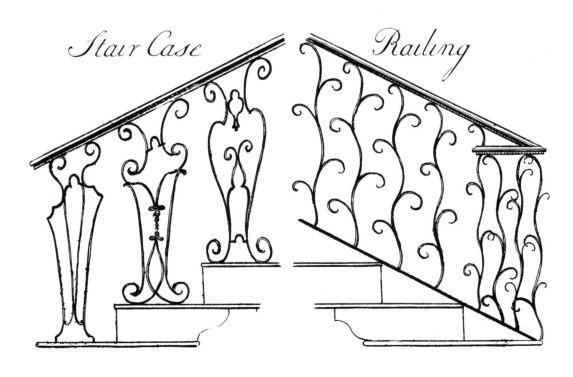

104

Stove   *Grate*

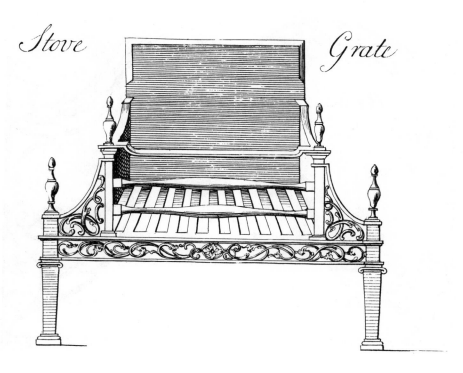

Stove   *Grate*

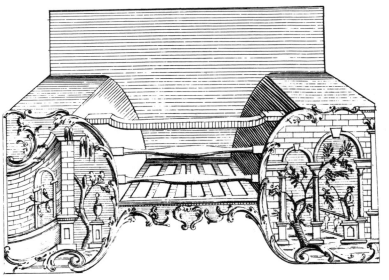

A Bath Stove

Brackets for Lanthorns